You Care Too Much

FREE YOURSELF FROM SOCIAL ANXIETY

Carl Vernon

ISBN: 9781999778750

First edition

As an international bestselling author and coach,
Carl helps people rediscover their lives.

Find more at **www.carlvernon.com**

Other books by Carl Vernon

Anxiety Rebalance:
All the Answers You Need to Overcome Anxiety and
Depression

Anxiety Rebalance:
All the Answers for Teens

Here's to you.

For deciding to free yourself from insecurity, self-doubt, social anxiety – and pretty much anything or anyone else getting you down.

May your days be full of joy and laughter.

Contents

Why do you care?

Social anxiety isn't everything you might think it is. Getting nervous in public and going the colour of a tomato around people don't touch the surface. You'll come to discover that these are superficial symptoms with a deeper cause. You're going to find out the *real* reasons behind social anxiety – so you can rip the problem out and completely transform the way you feel, not just socially, but in every waking moment of every day.

This book won't be like any other you've read on social anxiety and confidence. We're about to go directly to the source of the issue, so you can finally free yourself from the crippling and exhausting insecurity and self-doubt social anxiety causes.

I was crippled by social anxiety for over fifteen years. I was in a constant state of paranoia about what people were thinking. I'd replay conversations in my mind to make sure I hadn't said something stupid, and if I had (and I always had) I'd beat myself up about it for days. Worry about how I looked consumed me day and night. I suppressed my true thoughts and feelings, opting to stay silent rather than speak my mind. I didn't feel like I could be my true self. I went to great lengths to avoid embarrassment and being judged by others. And when I wasn't drowning in my negative thoughts, I was looking for things to buy that I thought would impress others (even people I didn't like!). My desire to be liked, and my fear of not fitting in, kept me well and truly trapped in the cycle of misery.

In this book, I'll continue sharing my experience and telling you about all the other fun ways social anxiety destroyed my life, but in the meantime, all you have to know that social anxiety goes deep. It's something that affects *all* of us. No one is immune.

Look at social anxiety like this. What if you woke up tomorrow morning to discover you were the last person on earth? Shyness, the need for approval from others, and anything else connected to social anxiety simply wouldn't exist, would they? Think about that for a second. Let it sink in. It's significant. I want you to start thinking about how much of your stress, anxiety, worry, fear, insecurity, doubt and discontent are due to you caring and worrying too much about what other people think – and how big a part this has to play in how you feel.

Being the last person on earth sometimes sounds like a nice idea, but short of an apocalypse happening, you are not the last person on earth. At the last count, there are 7.6 billion other people sharing the same space as you. You can run to the hills with your dog, Skip, who doesn't answer back and who shows you unconditional love, or you could go and live in a log cabin and dine on berries for the rest of your existence. Or you can choose to better manage how other people make you feel. For most of us, the latter option is the wisest and most productive choice. (If you still want to choose the dog and hills option, read on – you never know when someone might join you for a berry feast in your log cabin, making the skills you're about to learn useful.)

We're going to go on a journey of self-discovery – one that involves lots of eureka moments. These eureka moments transformed my life and my relationships with people. More importantly, they changed how I feel about myself. These discoveries came to me over the course of many years. I want to deliver them all to you in this book.

My journey started when I began to question the *real* cause of the crippling anxiety I'd experienced for fifteen years. Rather than continue to suffer in silence, I started to turn over rocks and challenge the status quo. Along the way, I uncovered some fascinating truths about social anxiety, including why we care too much about what people think, and why it affects us in such a debilitating way. It's so crippling, it can destroy lives. We can reach the later stages of our lives never having solved the social anxiety conundrum. In this book, I want to help you solve the puzzle and put the pieces together, so no matter how old you are, your quality of life will get better.

Changing things for the better requires a little more self-awareness and a change in mindset. This new mindset is what I call a 'can't care' mentality – which is something we're going to cover a lot more in this book, and something I'm going to help you achieve.

My 'can't care' mentality was building up inside me for years. It's hard to describe where it started. All I know is when I watched TV – especially ads, reality TV, soaps and anything relating to 'celebrities' – and when I used social media for personal use, I'd feel an underlying uneasiness. I felt a huge range of emotions, from frustration to despair, happiness to sadness, joy to anger, without giving myself time to understand or process what they were all about. I didn't appreciate or understand how much external factors like TV and social media were dictating my mood.

While I questioned my feelings and thoughts more, I began to notice patterns in my behaviour and other people's behaviour, including certain things they were saying and doing. As I dived deeper into finding the solution to social anxiety, I now recognise that these were all tell-tale signs of being snared by social anxiety (caring too much about what other people think). Summed up, that's what social anxiety is: **It's caring too much about what other people think.**

Worrying too much about what people think dictates how we feel, and act, on a day-to-day, hour-by-hour basis. Until we start becoming consciously aware of the impact this has, it will continue to govern our lives. If it weren't for my self-awareness, reflection and questioning, TV, social media and caring too much would still be governing my life today.

Have you ever made a decision or purchase, only to look back and think, 'What the hell was I thinking?' How about that smoothie maker that's still in the box in your cupboard? Or the fling you had with someone who now makes you shudder at just the thought of them touching you? It's likely it was **emotion over logic** that drove your decision. When you look back with hindsight, after a little more experience, time to reflect and logic, you can see how bad the decision was. At the time it seemed like the thing to do, but looking back it makes you cringe. You might also recognise this as 'I wasn't thinking straight at the time'. It was emotion and lack of logic that made your thought process skew-whiff. It's this type of thought process that keeps you trapped in social anxiety. When you learn to use logic *and* emotion, it not only transforms the way you deal with social anxiety, but also the way you make decisions. Using logic and emotion is something we'll cover in detail as we move forward.

When we go deeper into what all this means, you'll be shocked at how much you've been letting your emotion dictate your life (and lighten your wallet). More importantly, when I show you the tools and answers you need to change things, you'll be astonished by how different and more in control you feel. You won't only feel happier and more fulfilled; you'll handle relationships better and make better decisions. You might save enough money to go and do something you've always wanted to do. You might even have such a change in mindset that you transform the way you live your life.

The need for approval

Let's go back to the original question I asked in this chapter: 'Why do you care?' I know why. **Because *everybody* cares.** It's not just me or you who's been cursed. Caring too much about what people think is a plague on us all. An epidemic.

Feelings of social anxiety, insecurity and self-doubt cripple us all at times. They stop us from meeting new people and forming new relationships because we're scared of being judged and looking like a weirdo if we stop to say hello. The fear of change keeps us trapped in relationships and friendships that are no good for us. We repeat the same pattern of letting the wrong people into our lives (toxic people, people with narcissistic tendencies, people who let

6

us down) because we don't feel we can do better. Or we go back for more because we don't want to appear weak or like a failure in the eyes of others, or because we don't want to let someone down – even if it's at the cost of our own happiness.

These feelings of anxiety and insecurity stunt our growth and true potential. They prevent us from doing things outside the norm in case we're viewed as being 'different', or we fail and get the *I told you so*. Worst of all, they keep us trapped in a pattern of behaviour that means we're not comfortable being ourselves. We'll do anything to hide our true feelings by putting up a front that includes pretence and fakery. We do anything to avoid showing the world our flaws and vulnerabilities. We're led to believe that unless we're the very best at something, we're a failure. All these negative influences and beliefs are backed up by the people closest to us, such as domineering parents and judgemental 'friends'.

With every hour we spend living like this, we're going deeper into the hole of regret and dissatisfaction. Deeper into social anxiety.

All this time is being wasted. I urge you not to waste another second. What's the point of life if you don't feel that you can be yourself? Our imperfections, along with everything else that makes us individual, are to be embraced, not ignored. We don't have time to mess about with overwhelming insecurity and embarrassment. Life is too short and precious not to give yourself the opportunity to experience more mental freedom – the type of freedom we all have access to.

It's time to free yourself.

If you're not sure whether or not social anxiety relates to you, let me reassure you (or concern you, depending on how you look at it) that it most certainly *does* relate to you. The official definition of social anxiety is 'an intense anxiety or fear of being judged, negatively evaluated, or rejected in a social or performance situation'. We can all say we've been there. The need for approval from others is deeply embedded in us all. Just think about how much of your day is taken up by worrying about what other people think. It's a big problem. An epidemic. It's such a big and ongoing issue, it's no surprise that I still deal with the pointless worry it brings. But I'm glad to say I'm nowhere near as bad as I used to be. It's taken me thirty-plus years, but I've managed to reach a level where I care a lot less about what people think – and it's been life-changing. I'm just grateful I've been able to reach this new level of self-awareness. Most of us struggle to break the hold social anxiety has on us because of the obstacles it puts in our way. And there is no greater obstacle than worrying about what other people think of us and the need for their approval.

Picking up this book is one of the best decisions you've made recently because I'm going to help you reach the same level of self-awareness. When you do, you'll go about your business in a whole new way. Those feelings that have been plaguing you – including anxiety, insecurity and self-doubt – will continue to fall away. By the time you've finished this book, you'll have all the tools you need to turn your anxiety and self-doubt into authentic confidence and self-control.

We're going to do this by looking at social anxiety in a different way.

Apart from the usual blushing and stammering in public, how does caring too much and social anxiety manifest itself for you?

Do you find yourself being taken advantage of? Do friends borrow money from you, then not pay it back? Do your friends 'forget' their bankcard when you meet them for lunch? Have partners cheated or let you down, knowing that you'll take them back because 'you're nothing without them'? Do friends show up an hour late to meet you, only to chew your ear off for two hours straight without asking one question about how you are?

How is being taken advantage of connected to social anxiety? Don't people get social anxiety when they're doing a presentation or public speaking? Yes – but if you want to get better at public speaking, you may as well pick up one of the thousand books available on the subject of confidence. As I mentioned, social anxiety goes much deeper than that. You can become as confident as you like, but if you're not dealing with the root cause of your anxiety, you'll never fix it. Social anxiety isn't just present when we're under social pressure. Social anxiety is present at *all* times because it's how we feel about ourselves. We can't switch that feeling off. That means social anxiety permeates our entire lives – and, if we let it, it will do us some serious damage.

Some other ways social anxiety manifests itself is when you triple-check every conversation and human interaction you have to make sure you haven't said or done something stupid. If you spot something you regret, you'll punish yourself with persistent internal dialogue about how you're not good enough and never will be. Like that argument you had with your partner in 2010 – when you play it back in your head you beat yourself up because you regret not responding with the witty comeback you've just thought of. (Eight years later!)

When you care too much about what people think you won't leave the house unless you've spent an hour getting ready, even if you're just popping down the road for a pint of milk, in case you bump into someone you know. You'll take down pictures on your social media when you don't get the number of likes, shares and comments you think you should get. But probably the worst symptom of caring too much about what people think is the need to people-please. You'll spend most of your life living for everyone else, and forget about what makes *you* content and happy. Everyone else's needs and wants will take priority over yours. With such a mentality, you'll be destined to lead a substandard life.

Don't get me wrong – caring is a wonderful human trait. The world needs more people like you. The purpose of this book isn't to get rid of this fine quality; we're just going to tweak it a little. We're going to make it so you can continue to be a good, caring person, but not allow yourself to be taken advantage of. When you get the balance right between caring and being taken advantage of, your life will be much better. You'll be able to give with the sound knowledge you have the confidence and self-control to say 'no' when you need to. You won't allow your need for approval from others to overrule your own needs and wants. That's not selfish – that's smart.

The need for approval from others is so deeply implanted in us you'll think it's normal, so you won't pay much attention to it. It's only when you start feeling its damaging and crushing effects, including excessive insecurity, anxiety, worry and self-doubt, that you'll begin to question it. You'll reach a point where you ask yourself, 'Is all this worry about what people think really worth it? Is Sarah's comment about my new outfit that much of a big deal? Should her comment have caused this much crushing insecurity, to the point I want to rush back to the shop to get a refund? Or should I be able to wear what I want, and as long as I feel good and comfortable in it, silence the criticism from others and the conflict it causes in my head?'

'Is the massive self-doubt caused by Paul's opinion of my new business idea really going to stop me from doing it? Or should I go with the idea because I have absolute faith in my ability and believe my idea will work? What does Paul know? He's never done anything with his own life.'

'Is this crippling anxiety about the presentation I've got coming up worth all this time and worry? Or should I just trust myself and my capabilities, and be reassured by the fact that I'm going to practise and do my best – which will be good enough, no matter what happens? In fact, what's the worst that can happen?'

Sarah probably feels crappy about herself, so her bitchy comments about your outfit are a way for her to feel better about herself. Paul is scared of taking risks, which is why he's never done anything with his life. In his eyes, it's always a bad idea to take a risk. And the anxiety caused by the presentation is all in your head. It's based on other people's expectations which, when you look at them properly, are just the expectations you put on yourself. (We'll go into all this a lot more as we move on.)

All of this questioning is a good thing, and I hope you've started to question some of your limiting and false beliefs – especially when they're caused by other people. It's this type of questioning that helps us spot our bad habits – habits and behaviours we've been doing for some time that are no good for us. They're only good for making us feel trapped and fearful. These feelings keep us locked into the social anxiety cycle, making us do stupid and unnecessary things like buy things we don't need to impress people we don't like. The fear keeps us placed firmly on the floor, used every once in a while when someone needs to wipe their feet. (Doormat.) It keeps us obsessed with celebrities and reality TV because it becomes easier to live our lives through everyone else's. What a shit-show!

These cultures, the ones our society are built on, are so firmly fixed into our mindset (the way we think life is) that realising how much they influence our mood might concern you at first. But don't let it concern you; let it liberate you. If, for example, you connect the not-so-obvious dots between a celebrity fixation or another obsession and what it really means (the fear of facing your own emotions and responsibilities), don't continue the obsession. Instead, do something about *your* life. The same applies to anything that distracts you from what really matters: *how you feel*.

How much better off would I be if I didn't feel the need to think or act in this way?

A great question.

Most of us won't be able to wriggle free of social anxiety. We don't get close to asking the right questions about it because we're too wrapped up in our anxiety about what everyone else thinks and what everyone else is doing. Following the crowd puts us on autopilot, so we're not questioning or paying attention to the things that matter – like our mental and physical health. We're more interested in the finalists of the latest reality TV show than we are in finding something that will solve our feelings of unease and discontent. We might not feel that way when we watch the programme. It's designed to keep us distracted and entertained. But we do eventually feel it. We could be sitting at our desk at work, and all of sudden be overwhelmed with depression. We could be with friends and still feel lonely. All life needs and deserves substance, and these distractions only serve as short-term fixes. They don't fill the emotional hole that resides in us all.

These short-term fixes are damaging. The long-term effect is people in retirement homes being full of regret because they chose the short-term fix over the effort and bravery needed to listen to their true self. (That little voice you hear in your head that says to you, 'Why am I doing the same things, day in, day out?') When it calls out to you, it's easier to switch the TV back on and ignore it.

When you're brave enough to switch off the TV, put down your phone and switch off your computer, you fill that emotional hole with the good stuff – good stuff like being true to yourself, not living by other people's standards, ditching the need to people-please, and not caring as much about what people think of you. If you asked yourself, 'How much better off would I be if I didn't feel the need to think or act in this way?', what would the answer be? Mine would be 'So much better!'

Your challenge (if you choose to accept it) is to keep asking yourself questions. I want you to be your own game show host. Imagine yourself on *Family Fortunes*. Imagine saying to yourself, 'We asked 100 people why you care so much about what they think of you.' Hit the buzzer and be honest. Maybe you don't know the answer yet. If you don't, that's OK. Say 'I don't know'. Give yourself time. When you give yourself time and reflect, you'll come up with the answers. Answers like 'Because TV adverts and social media paint an unrealistic picture of how I should look' and 'Because I place too much importance on my friend's opinion.' The harder and more challenging the question, the more rewarding the answer. In other words, the answers to the right questions will be life-changing.

Along your journey, my job is to be your co-host. I know *Family Fortunes* didn't have a co-host, so you'll have to imagine a different game show. What about *Wheel of*

Fortune? That's a good example, because I'll be helping you reveal the letters and answers. However, answers and their meaning will be unique to you. 'Being true to yourself' means something different to everyone. The clue to whether or not you're progressing, and the thing to keep looking out for, is how anxious you feel. The more anxious you feel, the further away you are from being true to yourself. And vice versa. The less anxious you feel, the more you're being true to yourself. ('Being true to yourself' is a running theme throughout the book, and you'll find out what this means as we move forward.)

Asking questions and finding answers takes time and effort, but keep at it. You'll find, as you move forward, that new questions will pop up in your mind. Give yourself time to reflect and answer them. Don't worry if you don't come up with answers straightaway. You can always come back and read the book again if you need to. It has a deep enough message to warrant that. The mental freedom you get from the answers is well worth the time and effort. Caring a lot less about what people think and being true to yourself are truly liberating.

As you move forward, also try not to compare yourself to others. That's one of the quickest routes to becoming anxious. Rather than compare, pay attention to some of the habits, behaviours and beliefs of the people you know. When your self-awareness grows, you'll spot the patterns that keep people trapped in anxiety (fear). You'll see your friends and family falling into the trap. They'll say and do certain things, and you'll be like, 'Aha, I know why they think that!' For example, they may get anxious and make insecure comments about the way they look when they've seen a beauty-related advert. You can help them, but at the risk of sounding cruel, it's really up to them to help themselves. Have you heard the saying, 'Correct a wise man and he'll thank you, correct a fool and he'll hate you?' (Or something to that effect.) Not everyone wants a higher level of self-awareness. Some people might not be able to deal with it. In my favourite film, *The Matrix*, Morpheus tells Neo that not every mind can be freed from the matrix because it can be dangerous. I'll let you draw your own conclusion on whether gaining knowledge is a good or bad thing, as well as making the decision whether or not to share your knowledge. Personally, I say the more self-awareness the better. The more I've gained, the more I'm able to understand and control how I feel. But not everyone shares that view. You might come to discover that yourself.

If the people you know want to, they can go on a similar journey as you. You can help and guide them, but the decision to gain knowledge and increase their self-awareness has to be theirs. My focus is on you, and your journey.

It's important to remember that you can only help people who want to be helped. Don't get frustrated when you see other people falling into the same traps and fears. Just make sure you don't keep doing the same thing. It's important to remember that *you are your environment*. Your environment and the people you surround yourself with play an important role in who you are and how you feel. We'll also spend time on discussing ways to improve your environment.

This journey of discovery is your ticket to a level of mental freedom you've never experienced before. The freedom you get from being able to control insecurity, social anxiety and self-doubt is immense. It's so good, it should be prescribed as a medicine. It's more powerful than any anti-depressant on the market. Unlike a synthetic drug, you can't bottle it, so I can't hand it to you as the quick fix we all desire. But if you're willing to invest a little time and effort, I can give you the tools and answers you need to recognise the habits and behaviours social anxiety creates, so you can change them – and benefit massively from that change.

Why I wrote this book

I wrote this book for two reasons. The first is this need for approval from others we're all plagued with. Have you noticed how much of our time is taken up by the need to impress others? It's criminal. It was a major contributing factor to the crippling anxiety I suffered for over fifteen years. Don't get me wrong – there were lots of other factors that contributed to my anxiety, including having to grow up too fast, a stressful job I hated, being broke and continually questioning why I was doing what I was doing on an hourly basis (a symptom as well as a cause). But needing approval from other people was way up there on the anxiety Richter scale.

Since I've become consciously aware of how much I worried about what people thought, and have done something about it, I feel a hell of a lot better – about myself and other people. That debilitating feeling of shyness in social situations has gone. Intrusive thoughts about what people think come once a year rather than ten times a day. The deep urge to seek constant approval from everyone is no longer there to taunt me and dictate my actions. And best of all, I don't feel the need to buy things to impress people I don't like, including a house, sports cars, clothes and pectoral implants. I used to do all these things, and it just made me miserable. (Apart from the pectoral implants.) I found out that *respect for myself starts and ends from within*. And it feels good. I want you to feel as good.

The second reason I wrote this book is because I despise people who take advantage of good people. I hate bullies, abusers, manipulators: in short, toxic people. One of the side-effects of social anxiety is being extra-sensitive to all people, including the wrong types of people. That makes you more susceptible to being taken advantage of. When you can recognise toxic people and start dealing with them, your social confidence will soar. A little voice in your ear constantly bashing you about the way you look or the way you act can do serious damage to your self-esteem. When it's not there, you have extra time and space to focus on much more productive things, like finding some joy.

I've had the misfortune to be the victim of toxic people many times – people I thought I could trust. Since I've got better at spotting them and stopping them from affecting my life, it's improved my social anxiety tenfold. Notice I'm cautious not to say my social anxiety has gone. The theme of this book is that we *all* suffer from social anxiety at some point in our lives. A lot of that is dictated by new challenges, such as new people entering our lives. It's up to us to deal with the anxiety these potential challenges and people bring. I want to help you do that, just like I want you to help you deal with toxic people. I can't stop you from going through experiences and pain, and nor would I want to. We only know to avoid a snake when we feel the pain of its bite. Feeling the venom course through our veins gives us a pain that tells us, *no more!* It makes us determined to say 'enough is enough'. It won't always prevent us from being bitten again, but it will get us a step closer to where we want (and need) to be.

Who is this book for?

This book is for you. As well as being for anyone who might be dealing with social anxiety directly and specifically, it's for anyone going through its indirect and less obvious symptoms – things like being taken advantage of by less decent, immoral and underhand people. The book is for anyone who has considered living a life of solitude in the hills to get away from people – at least for a while. It's for the unfortunate people who were born to parents who thought they could mentally, emotionally or physically torture you because they believed they owned you – parents who don't care what psychological damage they inflict on their child.

This book is for the worriers and the insecure who want to stop feeling weak and vulnerable. It's for the socially anxious, who are tired of stumbling over words and feeling uncomfortable and scrutinised in public. It's for anyone who is stuck in a crappy relationship or job, too afraid to make a change. It's for anyone who is tired of being a doormat.

I don't claim I know all the answers. I'm not perfect. But I know that the extra level of sensitivity that naturally comes with social anxiety means that you are a good person, with good intentions. You wouldn't have picked up this book otherwise. You and I are similar. I share your values. I've worked extremely hard to increase my awareness and be a better human being, and to serve others. That's meant me sacrificing TV for reading, sugar for little to no sugar, meat for tofu, and social media for real life. When they said 'say no to drugs, kids', I obeyed. (I didn't include alcohol on this list. No one is perfect, right?)

When it comes to aiming to be a better human, you probably expect me to mention reading and socialising more, and cutting out drugs and alcohol. Why have I included meat and sugar? Like the others, meat and sugar are subjects that, I've come to discover, hold dark undertones. There's a strong moral argument for not eating animals, and cutting sugar means you decrease your chances of getting diabetes and other health complications.

My childhood was dysfunctional. As a homeless kid, I slept in a bus shelter. One of my first memories is seeing my father punch my mother so hard that her tooth came through her lip. I've been in foster care, where I was made to feel like an outcast. I've had a business go bust in a recession – a business I worked sixteen-hour days to build. I've lived with crippling anxiety for fifteen years, hiding it for ten years. *Poor me!* Nah, screw that. I only mention these things to highlight that I've seen and experienced both sides: from unaware and dysfunctional to self-aware and slightly more functional. I've had to work extremely hard – with no real guidance or help – to find the answers. Now, I'm in a good place where I can share these answers and my experience. I can show you how to be true to yourself, and how it feels when you care a lot less about what people think of you.

Caring less

'Caring less' and 'caring too much' are broad terms with little substance and meaning, so I'm keen to tell you what I mean when I say them.

By caring less, I'm not suggesting that you become an arsehole overnight and fight fire with fire. Life is not a game where the biggest douchebag (or 'King of the Douchebags') wins. Keep being the good person that you are. Just don't be a doormat or a people-pleaser any longer. Don't allow shyness, anxiety, worry, insecurity, self-doubt or the need for approval hold you back any longer. By continuing to be the good person you are, you stand a great chance of finding joy in life. With the new mentality I'm about to help you install, you'll be the same person, just more steely and self-assured. (And, more importantly, happier.) You'll run your own race – the only race that matters.

Being a doormat and being an arsehole are two ends of the scale; it's about getting the balance right. When you get the balance right, you can enjoy the fruits that life brings. You'll stop being walked over. You won't turn red when asked a question in public. You can give generously and help others succeed without being exploited. You will boost your self-confidence and self-esteem. You will manage and influence other people like a superstar. You will control your emotions and feelings in a way you didn't think was possible. And, best of all, you will end the continuous, pointless pursuit of approval from others. Sound good? I hope so.

How are we going to achieve all this? We'll do it in a number of ways – but, seeing as you've asked, I'll sum it up in one sentence.

By developing the skill of caring a lot less about what people think.

Where do you think most, if not all, your stress, anxiety, worry, fear, doubt, insecurity and discontent come from? What is the source? The real answer to this question is *you*. It's you who holds the key to how you feel. But for now, let's blame other people – it's not only easier, but it's also technically correct.

Stress, anxiety, worry, fear, insecurity, doubt and discontent come from your thoughts. These feelings are brought about by your internal dialogue (your thoughts). If you think an anxious or fearful thought, it's likely to make you feel anxious. And when you think happy thoughts, you're more likely to feel happy. This is not always the case; there are some other factors at play here. But for simplicity's sake, the point I'm making here is: **Your thoughts are directly related to how you feel.** That means you stand a good chance of regaining control over how you feel socially if you can start working on what you're thinking. And that's where this book comes into its own. I fully intend to get you thinking differently.

Our culture tells us what, where, when and how to do things, including how to look and act. You would have a very different life if you were born in Uganda compared to the USA. But you can't help where you were born. This doesn't mean you can't change: by going on a journey of self-discovery and increasing your self-awareness, you can change how you feel and shape your own destiny – wherever you were born, and whoever you were born to.

Your journey of self-discovery starts by becoming more aware of the external factors dictating how you think. Would you get as anxious or depressed about the way you look if you didn't see adverts telling you how you *should* look every two minutes? Perfect skin, perfect figure, perfect everything – it's all smoke and mirrors, designed to keep you buying products and trying to attain perfection. These manmade creations warp and influence our concept of what it means to be alive – to be human. A life of purpose isn't one where we run around like headless chickens trying to find a perfection that doesn't exist. A life of purpose is about being fulfilled and satisfied with what we have, and making the most of it. The best card players make the most of *all* their hands, not just the good ones.

How different would you feel if you had the strength to listen to and trust your instincts? If you could ignore your friend, who's telling you to apply for a safe job instead of starting your own company? What if you could ignore how many likes or comments your Instagram post gets, rather than feeling compelled to check it every ten minutes and delete it if it's not popular? What if, when your partner turns to you and says, 'You look fat in that', you could shrug it off, knowing he says things like that to deal with his own insecurities? (Or better yet, tell him to go find some other mug who will put up with his insecure BS.)

By telling you to care less about what people think, and helping you discover that people are at the heart of all your issues, I've just given you the magical cure. Why read on? All you have to do is care a lot less about what people think and you've made it. Easy. Right? You'll never have to read another crappy self-help book or watch another motivational video on YouTube to get you through the day again. You're fixed for life!

That is, until you're woken by your alarm – the sound that gives you instant anxiety because you despise your job. Or your boss kindly reminds you how useless you are, and belittles you in front of the entire office. Or your partner sleeps with your best friend. Or your child tells you they hate you. Or you excitedly open the email about the job interview you had last week. You were absolutely sure you got it, only to see the words *Sorry, but on this occasion...*

I'm not suggesting that you *don't* care about these things. Of course you should. As we move forward, you'll see that the solution doesn't lie in not caring; it involves changing how you deal with the way you care and the emotions involved in that.

Our lives aren't always black and white. If it were that easy, we'd all be living carefree lives, skipping and frolicking merrily, despite our flaws, faults and rejections. You only need to have a five-minute catch-up with a few friends or listen to some of the thoughts in your head to know that a carefree existence is far from most people's reality. But when you become more aware of how much you care, including about the pointless stuff, and start doing something about it, you'll make a vast improvement in the quality of your life. That is black and white, and it's as easy as choosing to read on.

Getting the balance right

Remember when I mentioned how important it is to get the balance right between being an arsehole and being a doormat? That's the last thing I want to cover in this chapter.

In nineteenth-century America, a confrontational young man would place a chip on his shoulder and dare another to knock it off. If the challenged man knocked the chip off his shoulder, a fight would commence. This is where the term 'having a chip on your shoulder' comes from. It describes a combative person carrying a grievance: in other words, an arsehole.

I don't want to give you a chip on your shoulder. When I say, 'care a lot less about what people think', I'm not suggesting you go to the supermarket in your Y-fronts, music blaring, chewing gum, your mouth wide open, walking down the aisles with a look on your face that says, 'So what?'. There is only a small part of this supermarket example I want you to take away and use – and that is to be more self-assured about yourself. The rest of this example, including the exposing of your undies, serves you no other purpose than to create enemies. Your life is much better when you have people on your side, which is why not caring at all is no good. There is little point living your life with a chip on your shoulder. Do that, and you become an arsehole.

Do you accept that people can, without doubt, be toxic at times? Do you also accept that *you* can be toxic too? If so, you're thinking along the right lines. And that's good, because change starts from within. There is little point in being one of life's victims and blaming everyone else, even if they have hurt you and contributed towards your mental breakdown. Until you start taking responsibility and stop playing the victim, change will continue to elude you. If you're happy to face your challenges head-on rather than run away from them, and accept your faults, even when things get tough, you're my kinda guy/gal.

Like I mentioned, we're not going to make that chip on your shoulder bigger. You don't need to read a book on how to hate the world – that is easy enough to do without a book. We're also not going to walk down the street carrying a banner, chanting 'We don't care what you think!' Stop caring as much about what people think is the backbone advice in this book, but it's more important that you are confident about *what* you think.

Don't be an arrogant fool who never listens to anyone and thinks he knows best all the time. Take on board people's views and opinions (including mine), and use the experience and endless knowledge at your disposal to make your life better. Accept constructive criticism graciously. Put your emotions and ego aside. There is value to be had from *all* feedback, even if it's not communicated very well. We'll all face criticism at some point. We can shy away from it by saying nothing, doing nothing, and being nothing, or we can face it like a champ and use it to make us better.

When I say 'care a lot less about what they think', I mean I want you to feel better about yourself. All that matters is what you think about yourself – your internal story and dialogue. That is what shapes how you feel and how you see the world. If you allow them, people will shape your world and how you feel for you. But if you use the tools I'm about to teach you, that won't happen to you.

As you progress, remember: It's not what people think that matters; it's what *you* think.

It's *genuine* confidence we're after, not this veneer quick-fix rubbish that only lasts a few days. When you combine your newfound genuine confidence with the ability to spot toxic people, you'll be set. You'll care less about what people think and you'll vastly improve how you feel about yourself, which will make you a hell of a lot happier and help you achieve more of the things you want in life. Best of all, you'll deal with social anxiety like a pro and nobody will mess with you. They may try, but after a few futile attempts, they'll move on to the next victim.

You'll come to discover that the biggest fear of all is the fear of people. When you crack that fear, the sky truly is the limit.

So whatever you want to achieve – whether it's to land your dream job, have untold wealth, bag your dream partner, tell your abusive partner to do one, put your parents, family and friends in line, or handle socially anxious feelings and thoughts – caring less about what people think and crushing your fear of people is the way to get it done.

If you're ready to make it happen, let's go.

Enjoy.

Carl

The difference between *can't* and *don't*

Did I mention that my crippling anxiety also made me housebound? I was in a seriously messed-up place. If you want all the gory details, read my first bestselling book, *Anxiety Rebalance*. Here, let's concentrate on the one thing that is going to help you manage your excessive caring, whether or not it comes with crippling anxiety.

If I were to say to you the one thing that took me from being housebound by anxiety to being able to get on stage and speak in front of thousands of people (just one example of the huge change that has happened in my life), it is simply this. **I *can't* care what people think.**

Notice, I say 'can't' here instead of 'don't'.

If I told you that I *don't* care what people think, it would be a lie. When you say you don't care, you're lying too. How can you not care? If we didn't care, we wouldn't be here. Of course we care. If I didn't care, I wouldn't have the desire to dedicate my life to helping others overcome anxiety. You wouldn't be reading this book because I wouldn't have written it. I wouldn't get out of bed, get dressed, or wash if I didn't care what people thought. Everyone cares! Me, you, the guy down the road, everyone! It's built in to us to care what people think.

We can strongly deny this instinct, but this fundamental truth will remain – we will *always* care what people think. We can deny it, or we can accept it and manage it better. My suggestion is that you accept it, because when you accept it, you can do something about it. Deny it, and it will eat you up. You'll want to retreat to that log cabin we've been talking about. Maybe you've already reached this point? I know I've been there many times. It's normal, especially when people have pissed you off. But think about what a solitary life really entails. The thought of having no central heating, internet or local shop would be enough to change most people's mind.

Yes, people piss us off sometimes. But look at the flipside. Think about the A&E doctor working three days straight, with no sleep, saving lives. Or the charity worker, taking two years out of her life to travel to another country to help build schools. Where there is hate, there is kindness. This is where the balance comes into play again. Mother Nature must have a sense of humour because you can find extremes at both ends of the scale. Where you find sociopaths who have no empathy, you also find people who have endless love and compassion for everyone. Extremes shouldn't influence how you feel. It's extreme to think you don't care, because you do. You might believe you don't care in that moment, but you do.

There is a severe mismatch between hating people and then expecting them to operate on you when you're dying. Or opening your laptop and trolling someone because you disagree with what they say. After all, you only get to use the laptop because someone invented it, along with the internet and the electricity to power it. All these things were created by other humans. It's too easy to get in a negative pattern of hate when you feel like you don't care, but remember, where there is bad there is good.

I *don't* care vs I *can't* care

I'm not sure if you've noticed, but the more you say you *don't* care what people say or think, the more you *do* care. (Go on. Be honest with yourself. There is no one listening to your thoughts.)

You might have met someone who makes a habit of saying that they don't care what people think. They will also say that they don't get on with other women, or that they don't bother getting involved with work colleagues because it's not worth the hassle. The truth is, these people are the ones who care the most! If they really didn't care, they wouldn't bother saying anything.

For the smart alecs who are sitting there thinking, 'You wrote a book about not caring about what people think, so you must care the most' – you're only half right. I used to care more than the average person, but now I've recognised how useless that is and worked on it, I've developed a new type of attitude I'm about to share with you. I see the light. I wrote the book because of how naive and stupid I used to be. I still care, but I do it in a new way. It's about being aware of how much you care so you can manage it better. This is where your new 'can't care' mentality will transform the way you deal with social anxiety.

I don't know how old you are, but I do know that, the older you get, the less you tend to care about what people think of you. And this is genuine. Have you heard the saying, 'the older you are, the wiser you get'? This genuine level of not caring as much about what people think is due to being wiser. Age doesn't always define how wise you are, but – generally – the younger you are, the more you care about what people think of you. So it's time to use the knowledge and mindset of the 'wise elders', and care less about what people think and more about what *we* think.

I want you to get in the habit of saying 'I can't care what people think', rather than 'I don't care what people think'.

Here's why. When you say you don't care, you're not only lying to yourself, but you're also developing a chip on your shoulder. These come with lots of hate and resentment towards other people. This type of attitude will only create enemies. Sure, have a few enemies. Life would be pretty dull without them. But make the reasons for your battles worthwhile. But if you have too many enemies, your life will be become unbearable.

Your life is much better when you have the right people on your side. They will help you create a life that feels good on the inside – not just one that looks good on the outside. You can only get the right people in your life and on your side if you care. That will attract other people who care. Like attracts like. If you don't care, you'll attract the same type of negative individual. When you care, you stand a better chance of attracting other like-minded people who will have a positive impact and influence on your life.

The mindset difference of 'don't' and 'can't' produces a very different outcome. When you say 'I can't care', you're saying that any opinions that others have of you are *their problem, not yours*. If it's their problem, it has nothing to do with you, so you can put it aside and move past it. You can't care about it. Just like you can't care about anything else that goes in other people's heads about you, including the insecurity they pass onto you via put-downs and negative comments. When people say and do such things, it's rarely personal. It's a reflection of themselves, and how they think and feel.

Think of your new 'can't care' mentality like regressing to your childhood. What were you like when you were a kid? I bet you didn't care that much about what people thought. You just got on with life. When you wanted to make friends, you went up to other kids and asked if they wanted to play. It was simple. If they didn't want to play, you went and found some other kids who did. It's only since you've developed inhibitions about how you should act as a grown-up that you stopped doing the things you did as a kid. Yes, we all have to grow up and take on adult responsibilities, but caring too much about what people think shouldn't be one of them.

If the childhood regression brought back bad memories (you won't be the only one), go and grab a tin of beans. Got it? OK, now hold the tin of beans in front of you so it sits on the palm of your hand. Depending how strong you are, you could probably stay like this for a while. The weight of the tin of beans isn't too much to bear. But what if you held the tin in that position for three hours straight? Or for a whole day? Or a week? What I'm getting at here is how we carry worry around with us. The tin of beans represents our worries – the worries caused by our insecurity. We can handle the worry for a short period of time, but after a while it becomes unbearable. Our arm goes dead and we can't use it. We have to be able to let it go. Saying that you don't care and pretending not to care will keep that tin of beans firmly on your palm. A 'can't care' mentality will allow you to let go and drop the tin (worry), freeing your mind for more of the good stuff!

Free yourself

What I'm talking about here is mental freedom. Mental freedom (a 'can't care' mentality) means not taking yourself too seriously. It's about being spontaneous, inquisitive, and being OK with a little more chaos (such as when things don't go your way). It's about enjoying the journey as much as the destination, appreciating that the only moment that is real is *this* moment, right now. It's the only thing that matters. We focus on the present rather than worry about the past and future.

Mental freedom is appreciating that you will be judged whatever you decide to do. You will make mistakes, which will sometimes lead to people saying 'I told you so'. If you have a 'can't care' mentality, that prospect won't stop you, and you'll try anyway. If you have a 'can't care' mentality, you'll start a business knowing how risky it is, and you won't be afraid to fail. The thought of risking some savings won't be as bad as the thought of being trapped in a job you hate for the rest of your life. If you have a 'can't care' mentality, you'll happily wear shorts when everyone else is wearing trousers. You might wear socks with your sandals because it's comfortable. (Or maybe that's pushing it?) You won't mind constructive criticism because you know it will help you grow – and you know that you will also criticise others because it is in *everyone's* nature to do so. When you can't care, you'll still replay conversations in your mind to check if you said anything stupid, but you'll be able to drop it (like a tin of beans) and move on rather than dwell on it. Your middle finger will slowly rise as you say these three magical little words:

I can't care.

As we move forward, you will come to discover that your new 'can't care' mentality is the best solution to all your anxiety, worry, insecurity and doubt. It will also help you deal with anything and anyone who tries to bring you down. When you *don't* care, you're kidding yourself and everyone else. When you *can't* care, you're fixed for life and everything it throws at you.

As well as developing a 'can't care' mentality, the ability to spot and deal with toxic people is an essential skill to keep you ahead of the game. The skills needed to do this are littered throughout the book. For now, let's continue to understand why we have this annoying need for approval from others. Once we've understood that, we'll knock it out of the park!

Led by fear

When it comes to worrying about what other people think, our decisions are led by fear. This fear that resides in us all holds great power. It will have you doing all sorts of things – like buying ridiculously expensive things you can't afford, including make-up, clothes, cars, jewellery – anything that you think will get you more respect and status. I call this having 'emotional holes'. We use all these material goods to try and fill these emotional holes. The problem is, they don't. And if they do, it's short-lived.

Before we get into this, I want to backtrack a little. It's important that you understand why you feel the need to do all this. It goes all the way back to your childhood. I'm the first person to say I hate the idea of my past, including my childhood, dictating who I am today. I'd rather be in denial about how much our early years define us. But if we're going to improve our future, we can't ignore the past entirely.

Let's regress

Regressing to childhood should be reserved for the therapy chair – and, if it were up to me, it would stay there. But whatever my opinion, our childhood plays a significant part in who we are today. Your childhood doesn't have to define you, but you'll be doing a lot of the things you do today because of the way you were brought up. The experiences you had when you were a child have shaped how shy or confident you feel around others today – in other words, how much social anxiety plays a part in your life today.

To some extent, we're all people-pleasers. A dominating factor in this is one of your parents (or a person you were close to when you were younger). No matter how good (or bad) your parents might have been, they weren't perfect. No parent is. Whether you're rich or poor, left-wing or right-wing, strict or tolerant, bad parenting is all too common.

Bad parenting leaves a gap in your development. Maybe your dad flew into a rage over the smallest things. Maybe he was hyper-competitive, forcing you into something you didn't want to do, like a sport or hobby. When you didn't win, he made you feel like you were worse than a loser – you were a let-down. Maybe you didn't feel that you could talk to your mum because she had her own problems. Maybe you didn't want to talk to your parents at all, because all they did was judge or misunderstand you. Maybe your parents leaned on you for support too much. Maybe your parents argued all the time, and that made you grow up wanting a quiet life. Examples of inadequate parenting are endless, and what they have in common is that they all lead to children developing social anxiety issues, such as people-pleasing. These behaviours carry on into adulthood. As a child, you had to react and adapt to your environment. It was the only way to survive.

Toxic parents rarely admit to having done any wrong. As an adult, you cling on to the hope that your parents will take some responsibility and will apologise – but if the apology never comes, you lose respect for them. That leads to resentment and bitterness towards your parents – feelings that make social anxiety worse.

It's also a no-win if your parents accepted you wholeheartedly and wrapped you up in cotton wool. Some of you might have had the 'perfect' upbringing, and because of this, wonder why you still can't have a conversation with a stranger. It's because being protected too much is as bad as being neglected. Knowing how to survive in dysfunctional circumstances creates a survival toolkit. These skills come in handy when your parents don't feed you. When you know how to survive, you can find someone else who will feed you. When you're wrapped in cotton wool and have everything your heart desires, you don't need these skills. That is, until you reach an age where it's socially unacceptable to still depend on your parents. It's too late then. Aged thirty-two, you'll still be thinking 'Mum used to deal with that. Dad paid for stuff like that.' When you move out of the family home, you'll feel like a lost fledgling. You'll avoid situations and scenarios that challenge you. Seeking a life with no responsibility can easily lead to social isolation.

I've used examples of very different childhoods to highlight the fact that, however you were brought up, it plays a part in who you are today. That includes how skilled you are socially, how functional or dysfunctional you are, and how happy or miserable you are.

I haven't used these examples to give you ammunition so you can blame your parents for your social anxiety for the rest of your life. As I mentioned, your childhood and past play their part, but they *do not* define you. If you're socially inadequate in your thirties, that's as much your fault as it is anyone else's. *You* can do something about it. There is little point in you playing the victim. Victims never get anywhere. Victims don't change. They're too busy blaming everything and everyone else for their shortcomings. Do you know someone who blames their parents – or everyone else – for everything that goes wrong in their life? They never get anywhere – they never move any further forward in life. They remain victims. Even if your childhood was bad-bad (yes, that's double bad), you have a choice. You can continue to play the victim and get nowhere. Or you can take responsibility and make the changes you're looking for.

Part of making any kind of successful change is understanding why the change is needed.

We don't need to get caught up in the detail or wallow in the past. Just understand that part of why you feel the way you do now is due to your past. Also understand that, if you let it, the past will own you.

Moving forward from the past starts with making the decision to do it, and taking action on that decision. When you've made that decision, only look back to check out the memories that help you grow – not the ones that keep you bitter and stunt your growth. Those types of memory keep you trapped. They produce emotions that cause us to wallow and stay in a victim-like mentality. Leave the past where it belongs and look in the direction you're going – forward.

Before we move on, here's a quick solution to people-pleasing, because I know how many of us are affected by it. It is simply this:

You can be pleasant without feeling you need to please.

That's how I'd sum it up. It's OK to say no. It's OK to disagree. Your childhood and your need to please others is long gone. You're an adult, and you can say no. That is your privilege. As long as you're not intentionally hurting anyone, there's no harm in doing what is right for you – and being OK with that. This is part of the 'can't care' mentality we are going to continue to develop.

The Joneses

The Joneses have a lot to answer for. Trying to keep up with them is never-ending! That's why I suggest that we ditch the climb and, instead, focus on ourselves and what we're doing.

Do you want to know the quickest route to becoming socially anxious and insecure? *Comparing yourself to others.* That'll do it every time. It will give you as much anxiety as you can stomach: 'He's got a newer car than me. His watch is more expensive than mine. Her boobs are so pert.' You can't care about what the Joneses are doing! If you do, you're destined to live a very unhappy existence.

Jewellery is probably one of the biggest emotional hole-fillers. I don't understand it. I know people who own £5,000 watches they hardly wear. It's nice to own nice things, but not when it gets you into debt, when it ends up stressing you out, and when you don't have spare cash because of it.

Rather than buy a watch for £5,000, wouldn't it be nice to have peace of mind with money in reserve if and when you needed it? Even if you can afford it, I think that £5,000 would be better spent on pretty much anything other than a piece of flashy jewellery bought with the sole purpose of impressing others.

Diamonds, as well as watches, catch some real suckers. Some of these diamond rings that cost an eye-watering amount look like the rings you get from the £1 egg machines at the seaside. (Do you remember those machines? You put a £1 in, twist the handle, and an egg drops down.) I say save yourself £9,999 and buy a £1 egg! Nobody would know the difference. (And if they did, you can't care.)

I was shocked to discover that there is actually a 'rule' for how much you should spend on an engagement ring. The rule says you should spend three months' salary. WTF! Who invented that rule? Um, lemme guess... it wouldn't be the jewellery manufacturers or retailers, would it? I mean, who makes up a rule like that?! If your partner asks whether or not you've spent at least three months' salary on a ring, and sulks if you haven't, I'd be questioning their intentions. There is nothing to suggest that how much a ring costs directly relates to how much a partner is loved. Actions speak louder than words, but in this instance, the only winners are the retailers – not the relationship.

I'm picking on jewellery here, but anything that depreciates rapidly can go into this 'useless' pile. Some pieces of jewellery and cars, for example, are sound investments. They hold or increase their value. These things are good. You get to own nice things and they don't cost you anything. It's just that these items tend to cost more than a house, so they're reserved for the super-rich. How do these people stay super-rich? They don't follow a 'rule' that says 'walk into your local jewellery store and buy a ring that will be worth less than half its value as soon as you walk out of the store.'

If you didn't waste money on useless purchases, think what you could do with the money you saved. Maybe you could invest it so you can retire a lot earlier. Or maybe it could go towards creating a memory or an experience, like a trip or holiday – something meaningful and worth its value.

Forget diamonds. Retire early! Go on more trips and holidays. Do more of the things you want to do – *now*. Widen your horizon – *now*. The world is a big place. Forget about the things that ultimately mean nothing and do nothing but feed pretence and fear. Leave the Joneses to follow pointless rules and make bad purchases. Do your own thing.

If you let it, your need to keep up with the Joneses will have you doing things you didn't think were in you. It will keep you trapped and in debt, wondering why your life isn't moving in the direction you want it to.

Social media

You've probably already heard about the pitfalls of excessive social media usage – things like it can lead to social anxiety and depression. But have you stopped to think about why? When you do, it's a bit of a no-brainer.

On social media, people like to pretend their lives are perfect. Unless you like flaunting your depression or you're having a bad day, it's common to want to represent yourself to others in the best light possible. That's why social media is such a crock. It's full of fakery and pretence. It gives the impression that all your friends are happy, all of the time, when that is just not possible.

When you're scrolling through your feed, you're bombarded with endless smiley faces. You're cheated by Photoshopped pictures. You're conned. Life doesn't work the way social media depicts it. It's little wonder we get so socially anxious and depressed when we spend too much time on social media. We're trying to live up to something that isn't real.

Social media companies hire people called 'attention engineers'. It's their job to make social media addictive. To do this, they borrow sneaky tactics from Vegas-style casinos. They want to make social media so addictive that people spend longer on there, maximising the profit that can be extracted from each user. When you're scrolling through your feed, you're basically pulling on a slot machine. The more times you pull, the more chance you have of winning. 'Winning' in this instance is a dopamine hit from game rewards, likes, comments and shares (which all equal approval from other people).

On social media, people care too much. They're being led to believe that everyone else's opinion counts. If they don't get enough likes, shares and comments, they think they're a failure. It's a dangerous way to live. Millennials are being led by fear – fear of missing out, fear of what everyone else thinks.

If you're going to overcome social anxiety, you seriously need to review how much time you're spending on social media. It isn't all bad. Like anything else, it's about being sensible. That means using it in moderation. It becomes unhealthy when you become addicted – when you feel like you can't spend time away from it. It becomes an issue when you use it to get social gratification. When you find yourself thinking and acting like this, it's time for a social media detox. You might like the detox so much that you choose to spend less time on social media. However much time you choose, remember the 'attention engineer'. Are you going to keep them in a job, or are you going to free yourself?

Do your kids and teens the same favour, and free them too. Educate them about the potential pitfalls of social media. You don't have to get preachy about it. I hope I haven't come across like that either. (See, I do care what you think.) If you're not a millennial, you'll know what it's like to live without social media. Kids and teens today don't. As I mentioned, it's addictive. So use kid gloves and be patient.

The DP rule

In my bestselling book *Anxiety Rebalance*, I exposed our two greatest fears. They are the fear of **D**eath and the fear of **P**eople. I call this the DP rule. You can link all your fears and worries back to these two things. Try it. Write down all the things that are worrying you right now and the reason for that worry. For example:

Fear: The presentation I have to deliver in front of my colleagues next week.

Why do you fear it?: Because I don't want to make a fool of myself in front of everyone.

If you continue to take these worries back to their source, they will always lead back to the fear of death or the fear of people (or both). It's the latter fear we're concerned with here.

Do you know what our number-one fear is? Death? No – that normally comes about fourth on the list. Spiders? No – they also come a little further down the list. I gave you a clue in the example I used above. The consistent number-one fear we have is public speaking. If you think about it, it's just another way of saying that our number-one fear is *other people*.

We are consumed by what other people think of us. It governs our day. It dictates how we live. It defines our mood. Before we do anything else, we have to find out why this is, so we can understand what is really driving our decisions – then do something about it. The good news is, I can explain it easily and quickly.

Human beings have fundamental needs. The need for approval from others is implanted in us from birth, which is why, in one way or another, we seek approval from everyone we meet. If we didn't have this instinct, babies would be abandoned, relationships wouldn't form, and we'd all be psychopathic sociopaths on a rampage.

Not convinced? I knew you wouldn't be. That's why I want you to pop to your local shop wearing just your undies. No? Don't fancy that one? Too cold? OK, I've got another one for you. The next time you go out, I want you to walk up to the first big burly bloke you see and give him a big kiss. (If you're an attractive female, he might like that, so this won't work as well. This example tends to work best when you're a burly bloke yourself.) You're unlikely to do it – not only because you want to keep your teeth, but also because it wouldn't meet his approval. He wouldn't perceive this to be 'normal' behaviour. The same goes for taking a trip to the local shop in your undies. Most of us wouldn't do it because other people wouldn't approve. You would get stared at. People would snigger and comment. You would feel incredibly insecure. All of this potential embarrassment helps to keep us from doing things that aren't perceived as the 'norm' – things outside our comfort zone. They keep us from killing each other. People who go outside this normality are usually locked up in prison or in a padded cell for their warped view on 'normality'.

Our culture dictates what is normal and what isn't. Most of us feel secure when we conform with that culture – when we follow the crowd. That is how trends are set. Bell-bottoms might have made you look cool in 1970, but if you wear them today, you'll look like a crazy fool who's been digging around in his granddad's wardrobe. But if a big fashion company decided that bell-bottoms were back in fashion, everyone would start wearing them again, and you'd no longer be a crazy fool because the masses would say that bell-bottoms are OK. (Thank you, Granddad.)

It takes a lot to go against the norm. People like Rosa Parks are one in a million and define what I'm saying here. Rosa was the lady who refused to give up her seat on the bus to a white man in America in 1955. At that time, it was against the law for an African-American person not to give up their seat to a white person. Today, that concept sounds medieval. But it took people like Rosa to go against the norm to change it. She literally had to put her life on the line. Rosa had a 'can't care' mentality, and that helped her to see right from wrong, even when her culture was saying something different. If Rosa had cared more about what other people thought than she cared about doing what she believed was right, nothing would have changed.

This fundamental need for approval from others has its upside and downside. The upside is, it keeps us living in a relatively harmonious society. Barring the odd world war, humans are generally a peaceful bunch. If we didn't need others' approval, the film *The Purge* would be an accurate portrayal of life. We would need to live behind big gates with a gun close to us at all times. (Thinking about it, some of us already live like this.) The downside of our need for others' approval is everything we are trying to combat in this book, including, but not limited to:

- Insecurity
- Worry
- Doubt
- Anxiety
- Stress

- Discontent
- Anger and rage
- Depression
- Paranoia
- Toxic behaviour
- Being a people-pleaser
- Lack of direction
- Being a doormat
- Lack of purpose
- Being broke
- Uncontrollable debt
- A constant feeling of uneasiness
- Absolute fucking misery.

If any of this list rings true for you, it's time to break the cycle.

Break the cycle

Due to external influences such as adverts and social media, many people today believe they're not good enough. They're influenced to believe this because it keeps their hands in their pockets. When we buy things, it's good for the economy. It's time to break this cycle, refocus, and begin reconnecting with ourselves. It's time to dismiss the meaningless stuff and focus on the good stuff. That starts with believing we are already good enough, just as we are.

Social anxiety attacks you as soon as you wake up. If you're a smart phone user, there's an 86% chance you'll wake up and go straight on your phone. You'll check your social media, news and emails as soon as your eyes open. All of this gives you instant anxiety and stress.

Social media has been proven to increase anxiety and depression. If you have any doubt about its effects, Google it for yourself. You might come across people like Jaron Lanier. Jaron is regarded as one of the founders of virtual reality, and was very much part of the Silicon Valley scene. He now exposes the sneaky tactics used by social media platforms and promotes public awareness of the dangers of social media, presenting sound reasons for his views.

The news and emails are just as bad for your mental health as social media is. Generally, the news is negative. And most emails sent to us are because someone wants something from us! Faced with so much negativity, we go into an immediate 'reactive' state of mind – a thinking process that leads to worry about who we are, the work we do, and what other people might be thinking. Checking our phones isn't the most productive way to start our day.

If it isn't the beauty industry, celebs, TV ads or social media reinforcing how imperfect and ugly we are, it's the people closest to us putting us down. 'Why are people so cruel?' you might ask. Because people need an outlet for their own insecurities – insecurities we all have, you and me included.

There is no doubt you've put someone down because of your own insecurities. I know I have. This doesn't necessarily make you a horrible person (unless you make it a habit). It makes you human. We want to feel good about ourselves, and sometimes that means making others feel bad. When you arm yourself with this knowledge, and become more aware of it, you might choose to put people down less often. It might become apparent that you don't need to do it any longer to feel good about yourself. When you hear one of your friends doing it, rather than reacting, you might choose not to react because you know it's just their own insecurities coming out.

The beauty industry and the celebs that get paid to represent them need you to feel bad about yourself so you go and buy their product … to help you feel better about yourself. Your insecurity is a good thing for these guys. It means pound signs. A crude example of how this works looks like this:

A TV ad about cosmetic surgery pops up.

You immediately feel insecure and compare yourself to the model on TV.
(Comparing yourself to others is one of the quickest routes to becoming anxious and insecure.)

You fear that you will never look as good as the model.

You consider getting a loan for the procedure, only to realise you can't afford it.

Insecurity, fear, resentment, discontent and anger build up inside you.

Your child comes home from school and you need to release all those negative emotions.

You feel insecure, and manifest these emotions in a toxic way, like making a nasty comment to your child.

Your child thinks this is how life works, and treats her friends in a toxic way.

She grows up and treats her kids in the same way.

The cycle continues.

I know, I know. I've taken a TV ad all the way to creating a vicious cycle that ruins a family. I did say it was a crude example. It is extreme, but I'm just highlighting how the cycle works. It's not just the TV ad about cosmetic surgery. Think how many adverts you see on a daily basis – and not just on TV. A friend might post on social media that she's just had a nose job, a celeb might post pictures of her new buttocks. There are billboards on the way to work, and shops selling the latest shoes. Your neighbour's bought a new car. It's an endless barrage of how we need to change in order to fit in, and a constant pressure to buy the next thing.

It's time to break this cycle, for the sake of your well-being *and* your wallet. For the sake of your family and future generations.

Cycles tend to be more powerful when they're perpetuated by a group of people, such as a family. Children learn to behave in the same way that their parents behaved. So if your dad is toxic and insecure, it's likely he'll be passing those traits on to you. And so on. No one learns any different, and the cycle continues.

You have an opportunity to break this cycle, today. It starts and finishes with you.

If you want a better cycle for you and your loved ones, you have to feed it with something you don't mind coming out of the other end. If you don't want toxicity, don't feed the cycle with toxicity. If you want respect, feed your cycle by *giving* respect. Do that, and you'll get more respect coming out of the other end.

Now do you see what I mean when I say the cycle starts and finishes with you? It's up to you to take control of what you're putting into your cycle. If you eat junk food all day, it will produce a cycle of junk. If you watch mindless TV all day, including ads, it will lead to anxiety, insecurity, resentment, doubt, fear and anger. This is precisely why I don't watch TV any more. Don't get me wrong; I'm not a hippy with no TV in my house. I still have Netflix and a few other on-demand options. But previously, I had the lot – satellite TV with over a thousand channels, most of which I never watched. I'd come home from work, plonk myself down on the sofa and start flicking through all the channels. I'd spend more time doing that than actually watching something!

When I babysat recently for some friends, I appreciated just how much time I had wasted. They had satellite TV, and I found myself flicking through the channels, up and down, until I stopped myself and realised how dumb it was. TV ads came on, and they made me feel instantly angry and inadequate. I rolled my eyes at how manipulative they were. I wouldn't have appreciated any of this if I hadn't been desensitised by not watching them consistently. I'd have accepted those negative emotions as normal, and continued making those pointless purchases.

Like I say, I'm not a hippy. I have a TV. But I get to pick and choose what I watch, minus the ads! (And the feelings of inadequacy.)

It's not just time and money I've saved by not watching TV. It's been a life-changing experience. I cannot begin to describe how much better I feel. My social anxiety, fear and insecurity are much lower. Plus, I have so much more time to do the things I enjoy, like read and write. In about three days' worth of flicking through all those satellite TV channels I can read an entire book (or listen to an audiobook).

I didn't write this book to dictate to you what you should do. I don't wish to set some cult-like rule that says TV is evil and should be banished. I just want to get you to think about the external factors that influence how you feel, including TV. If you start to feel that it's having a detrimental effect on you, do something about it. You don't have to watch it just because you have it, or because your family is watching it. You have a choice. You always do.

You're in control

There are two simple things that will make a world of difference for you when you adopt them: (1) Being slightly more conscious about the things you say (both to yourself and others), and (2) Paying a bit more attention to what is influencing how you feel.

When you feel negative emotions bubbling up, you can put a stop to them by being aware of where they are coming from. For example, if you get anxious after watching a TV ad but never fully understand or appreciate why, you now know it's the ad. It's been designed to do that so you go and buy the product to make yourself feel better. With this new level of self-awareness and self-control, you no longer need to go and buy the product. An even bigger bonus is you'll automatically stop passing on your insecurity to others, including your kids. You will become much more self-confident and less socially anxious. That will be enough to stop the cycle dead.

Like I mentioned, forget about trying to get others to break the cycle for now. The beauty industry, celebs, TV ads and social media – all these things will always be popular, and they will always play their part in the cycle. That's just the way it is. It's our culture, and cultures don't change overnight. But you can.

The same goes for trying to change toxic people. Leave them to it. Maybe they'll change in the future. Maybe they won't. Who cares? Move on. Don't worry about what others are doing – this time is dedicated to you.

Remember, the only person you can control is you.

When all of this clicks for you, if it hasn't already, it will frustrate you to see others being trapped. You will see first-hand how manipulative advertising is. You might get fed up with trivial 'news' stories about celebs because, quite frankly, who cares? They have zero relevance to you or your life. You might want to switch off your social media for a bit. When your friend puts you down, rather than get angry, you might smile or be sympathetic, knowing that the root cause of their put-down is their own insecurity. It's difficult, but try not to be smug or judge. Remember that you were once in their position, reacting to all insecurity with more insecurity and allowing the negative cycle to continue.

Moving forward with your new 'can't care' mentality, you will be able to decide how something or someone makes you feel and what you want to do with that feeling. If you buy a nice thing, it will be because you want to do it – not because you're being told to do it or you're being influenced or manipulated. Your new 'can't care' mentality will help you spot whether or not someone is acting insecurely (through habit and naivety) or whether he or she is trying to hurt you. You need to deal with these two types of people differently, and you'll discover how to do it in later chapters, including 'A turd in the punchbowl'.

For now, let's continue to develop our 'can't care' mentality by embracing the fact that nobody cares.

Nobody cares

How do you feel when you say (or think) 'nobody cares'? Depending on how you view it, it might make you sad, or it can set you free. The feeling you get depends on your mentality when you say or think it. The aim here is for your new 'can't care' mentality to liberate you. I want you to start getting ecstatic about the fact that, when it comes to it, nobody really gives two shits.

Fear of failure

In life, we do our best not to fail. This is mostly down to us not wanting anyone to see us fail. It would embarrass us if others see our business go down the pan, our marriage fail, or our pants fall off while playing tennis. When we look into this a little deeper, it highlights some big concerns. The largest concern is the fact that we stop ourselves from doing things because of what *everyone else might be thinking*. I want you to think about this. Not just for a second, but for as long as it takes to realise how stupid it is. We're basically stopping ourselves from doing things that are potentially life-changing because of what someone *might* think about us.

Until we start to realise how much worrying about what people are thinking about us influences how, what, where and when we do things, we'll continue to be locked up. We'll put off things that could be good for us because of what someone else *might* think.

Until you achieve a stronger 'can't care' mentality, you're at risk of social anxiety. Why? Because you'll always be too sensitive and susceptible to what other people are thinking. You have to listen to yourself and trust yourself. It was you who put your life together. Ultimately, it was you who got through your problems. Don't destroy your life because you believe everyone else's criticism. Listen to feedback, but do it constructively. Do it with the self-confidence you had when you were solving your problems.

A fear of failure (caring too much about what people think about you failing) will make or break you in anything you do. Let me ask you a question: Who here hasn't failed? No one, right? Everybody has failed at some point. It's just that some people are better at masking their failures than others. But hiding failure isn't necessarily a good thing either. It's a weakness. The more you're willing to put your failures out there, the stronger you will be. When you say to the world,

'I'm going to do this and accept the prospect of failure. If I fail, I'll keep going and come back stronger', you are strong and resilient. That's a great mindset to have. You wouldn't want to be in competition with anyone who had this mindset. (Yourself included!)

When you're not afraid to fail, nothing can stop you.

Even better, when you see failure as a way to learn and an opportunity to grow, you might even start embracing it. It's true: it's only through failure that you learn the hard lessons, the type of lessons that stick and make you who you are today. If things went right all the time, not only would life be incredibly dull and boring, but you'd never truly learn anything of value. You can guarantee that anyone who has a successful and fulfilling relationship, business or career has failed in others before it.

If you're going to keep developing your 'can't care' mentality and free yourself from social anxiety, you have to accept your failures and be willing to put them out there. You have to radically change what you think failure means. The same goes for rejection, which you can lump in with failure.

Fear of rejection

Why do you think so many people drink alcohol? It helps us lose our inhibitions. Sam would never have plucked up the courage to speak to the girl at the bar if he hadn't drunk three pints beforehand. And thank goodness he did. She and Sam got married a few years later. (The marriage ended pretty quickly. Well, what do you expect when you meet someone at a bar?)

Doesn't it make you wonder what other opportunities you're missing out on because of your inhibitions? I'm not saying the solution is to become an alcoholic. That will cause its own problems. The odd glass of red every now and again won't do us any harm. (I have to say that, otherwise I sound like a hypocrite.) Hey, it even reminds you what it feels like to be footloose and fancy-free every now and again. But alcohol isn't the solution, I'm afraid, and nor is any other drug, legal or illegal. The answer lies in seeing rejection for what it really is.

Rejection and failure are a healthy part of life.

Winning comes with lots of rejection. It comes with lots of failures. We normally have to kiss a few frogs before finding our Prince Charming. He won't just turn up at your door one day. And he usually doesn't appear until you've dated a few frogs...

The only difference between the top seller in the sales office and the guy getting sacked is their ability to expect – and handle – rejection. Both of these guys are getting rejected by prospective customers left, right and centre, but the top seller thinks, 'If I get rejected, I'll handle it. Well, the product probably isn't right for him. I'll move on to the next prospect.' Compare this to the guy getting sacked: 'But he said he didn't want my product. That must mean I'm a complete failure. I'm going home to sob into my kebab.'

We either face and accept rejection and move on, or we get stuck on it. Remember this the next time you want to succeed or be the best at anything. Look at improving your skill set in the area you want to improve, but don't forget about improving your *mindset*. This means being prepared for rejection. When you can develop both of these skills, you'll be the best.

You can relate this example to anything. Being a top seller. Finding a partner. Making friends. Finding a job. Starting a business. Anything. Rejection looms everywhere, as does success. It's how we handle rejection that matters. That comes down to our internal story, and being aware of how much this story is influenced by other people. The top seller cares what people think just as much as the guy getting the sack, but he doesn't allow others seeing his rejection to stop him from making the next call. He doesn't get stuck in the rejection. He moves on and picks up the phone while the other guy is still sobbing into his chilli sauce. The person willing to accept that they'll have to kiss a few frogs before Price Charming comes along is more likely to find their prince – and really appreciate the relationship when they do.

I know how it feels to be affected and influenced by rejection. It's like each time you're rejected, it takes a tiny piece of your soul away, until you reach a point where you can't handle it any more. That is, unless you start changing how you feel about it. A big part of this change is not being so bothered about what others think of your rejection. If you can develop a 'can't care' mentality, you'll handle rejection in an entirely different way – and you'll be able to face it more often. By discovering all the tools and answers in this book and, more importantly, putting them into action, you'll build an internal steelwork that makes you feel stronger than you ever have. When people snigger and make comments, it will push you forward rather than hold you back. It's through this mindset shift and action-taking mentality that rejection won't hit you as hard. That tiny piece of your soul will remain. When it stays where it is, your success will grow organically and your social anxiety will drop.

Some people will want to see you fail. It makes them feel better about their own failures – not so alone. When your marriage isn't doing well, seeing Claire's marriage fail gives a form of relief and comfort. *Thank goodness it's not just me.* This doesn't necessarily make you callous. It just makes you human. Failure and rejection can be solitary places. It's nice when others join you.

The next time you're rooting for someone to fail, you know it's not just because you're a horrible person. You just want someone else to feel how you're feeling. But (and there is a big 'but') it's important not to get into this habit. It can easily lead to an increase in callousness – and that would make you a horrible person. It's a much healthier mentality when you're happy with your friends winning, even though you want to win yourself.

Become more aware of how you feel when you are rejected. Remember, rejection isn't that much of a big deal. Be reassured by the fact that, if you're facing rejection on a regular basis, it means you're growing. And that's good. There is nothing worse than stagnating. I don't know about you, but I'd rather have a life of trying, and being rejected a few times, rather than not trying at all – especially if not trying is down to what other people *might* be thinking.

All eyes on you?

I started this chapter by saying that, when it comes to it, nobody really gives two shits. And it's true.

Do you really think most people care whether you win or fail? Do you think they care about what you're doing if it doesn't impact their lives directly? Maybe in the very short term they care, and perhaps your parents and a few friends do, but apart from that, nobody really cares about what you're doing (or not doing).

All eyes are *not* on you.

Even if you're a world-famous billionaire, failure ends up being old news. Yesterday's newspaper is tossed away and people move on. Our attention spans are short. Things are constantly evolving, and we're always looking for the next trend. That's why bell-bottoms aren't in fashion any more, and why you're up to an iPhone X, or whatever it is now. An iPhone 4 just doesn't cut the mustard any more. Very soon the next iPhone won't, either. This means that your last failure will be forgotten as quickly as it happened. So don't get stuck on it, because no one else will!

Whatever you choose to do today – that thing causing you anxiety about what people are thinking – will very soon be old news. People will forget all about it (and you). When you look at it like this, isn't it a shame you're allowing all that fear of failure and rejection to hold you back?

When it comes to it, nobody cares apart from you, and I suggest you embrace that fact. It should be liberating. It should free you from social anxiety. It means you get a shot at doing what you *want* to do, rather than getting up every morning to do that dead-end job. Instead, you can follow your calling without worrying about what your boss and colleagues think. It means you can end your abusive marriage, because your family were never going to understand why you left him anyway. You can sell your possessions, get rid of all the emotional baggage, and sail around the world, knowing that your friends think you're mad. Mad? Being chained to a desk at work, I suggest, is much madder than spending your days watching the sun's rays glimmer and bounce off the sea as you set sail. No, my friend, succumbing to a 9–5 existence is, when analysed, much more insane than taking a chance on a dream.

I don't know what is right for your mental state and well-being, and I don't know what opportunities you have that you're missing out on. I'm not suggesting that you need to do something crazy to get a kick out of life. I just want to show you that all eyes are *not* on you. Don't miss out on finding joy because you fear what somebody *might* be thinking. Let your 'can't care' mentality take you where you want to go.

Remember that, whatever you choose to do, people will continue to go about their business. It won't affect them. Please, take this knowledge and do something with it. Let it free you from social anxiety.

Self-awareness

The one thing I'd like you to take away from this book is how to be more self-aware: more aware of your 'self', your environment, the people in your life, your decisions, and why you're doing what you do. Why? Because self-awareness is the key to you making the changes you want, and sticking to them, and one of the keys to overcoming social anxiety – and any other form of anxiety.

You'll hear me mention self-awareness a lot. I want to clarify what I mean by it. Put simply, self-awareness is the *ability to question*. It prevents you from being led by the masses and doing what you've always done. It doesn't mean looking in the mirror every day and overanalysing what you do and say. Self-awareness is simply the ability to ask yourself, 'Why did I do that?' and 'Why am I putting up with that?' (for example, when you're putting up with a situation that makes you unhappy). Without self-awareness, you can't change the situation.

The ability to question ourselves starts when we're young. But that doesn't mean we always use this ability. You can have the best, most advanced tools in your toolbox, but if you don't know how to use them, they're useless. Some of us knew we had this tool (the ability to question) early on in life, and this gave us a distinct advantage. Many of us didn't, simply because we weren't shown or told how to use it. This could be due to lots of things, such as our parents and environment. Let's start there.

The game is rigged

We aren't born equal, that's for sure. The game is rigged. Some people are born with bad parents, and others get a clear mental, emotional and financial advantage by having good parents. Nevertheless, none of the disadvantages you may have been born with should get in the way of you changing who you are today. You should still be able to reduce your social anxiety.

The best example I can give to demonstrate the difference between self-awareness and lack of self-awareness (also known as naivety) is from the film, *The Matrix.* When you're naive, you're plugged into the matrix. You walk around without a real purpose, allowing everyone else to dictate your feelings. You go from one day to the next, existing, without questioning your 'self', your environment, the people in your life, your decisions, and why you're doing what you do. When you're self-aware, you're unplugged from the matrix. You're living and aiming to thrive. External factors, including what people do and think, have less of an impact on you. You have a higher level of self-esteem and self-control, and that leads to a richer and more fulfilling existence.

I would love to offer a magic answer when it comes to gaining more self-awareness, but I really don't have one definitive answer or solution. No one does, or ever will. It's too personal to you. Too subjective. You can Google self-awareness and study things like good habits. This is all good. *All* useful knowledge is good. But the type of self-awareness I'm talking about here, the type built over time and through experience – that self-awareness can't be forced, handed to you on a plate or bought at your local shop. The good news is, it can be developed just by becoming more aware about being more self-aware. (Yes, you read that correctly.) To become more self-aware, you first have to be more aware. You have to reflect, and question. You have to want to gain knowledge and be open to learn from others.

What I'm saying here is based on common sense. How can you become more self-aware if you're not aware you need to change in the first place? It's like wanting to be a better person, but having no clue why you might be a bad person. How do you know what to change?

When I was plugged into the matrix, I wasn't aware. I was naive. It's only since I've become more self-aware through knowledge and experience that I've appreciated the *need* to be more self-aware – and enjoyed the benefits it has brought me. Some people realise they need to be more self-aware through spiritualism, meditation or religion. It doesn't matter where you get your self-awareness from as long as the tools being used aren't controlling or manipulating you. When we realise we would benefit from a greater level of self-awareness, it can increase our vulnerability and susceptibility. We might reach out to institutions that, on the face of it, appear as though they are aiding us. In reality, they are dictating what, where, when and how we should do things. This is no better than being trapped in the matrix. You'll know you're becoming more self-aware (in the right way) when you become less socially anxious and you feel more true to yourself. (Something we're going to cover in a second.)

The person you see when you look in the mirror today is very different to the person you were ten years ago. Imagine how much better you could handle your anxiety today if someone had told you ten years ago to be a little more self-aware, to ask yourself why you feel the way you do. Self-awareness gives you the ability to question yourself when you're caring too much and suffering from anxiety, for example. Self-awareness provides you with the strength to look and act how you want, and be OK with that. (As long as you're not hurting anyone.) But let's not live in regret. We can't time travel or change the past. Let's decide from now that you're going to make an effort to be more self-aware, so you can experience all its marvellous benefits, including handling your social anxiety better. Let's start by being more true to ourselves.

Be true to yourself

I used to run a small business. At its peak, I employed twelve people. I hated it. I came to discover that employing and managing people just wasn't for me. The giveaways were the crippling anxiety and stress that hit me as soon as I woke up, and the never-ending illnesses.

I've got friends who run businesses and they're miserable. They go home in the evening, complaining about their staff, ready to break down or fly into a rage at any second. When I suggest to them that the hardest part of their job isn't their job at all, it's managing people, they find it a hard concept to grasp. They typically revert to two points of view: (1) If they abandon what they've worked towards, they are a failure, and (2) Things will change if they just give it time. On the first point, you have to get off a ship that is sinking, even if it took you years to build it. On the second point, I'm going to refer to my favourite saying by Albert Einstein on the definition of insanity: doing the same thing over and over again and expecting a different result. **Nothing will change unless you change what you do.**

Again, you can relate this example to all major factors in your life, not just business. Being stuck in a situation you don't like could also mean a job or a relationship. If you're in a situation that means you're not being true to yourself, it's up to you to change it.

Part of becoming more self-aware and being true to yourself is not sweeping problems under the carpet. When you do that, problems just end up growing until they become monsters. You need to face your fear head-on (including the fear of change). In relation to social anxiety, being more self-aware could mean not avoiding social situations to gain short-term comfort. That short-term comfort is short-lived. The problem just keeps getting worse the more you avoid doing it. Self-awareness will tell you that you need to take action and expose yourself to social situations if you want things to get better. And that's the solution: **avoiding avoidance**. Rather than say no, say yes more often, even when it feels uncomfortable. It's only through exposure and experience that you'll change a situation and, in turn, change how you feel.

In the final chapter, we'll cover taking action in detail. Action is the best tool I can give you. It's the only tool that solves problems. I haven't left it until the end of the book because I want you to wait or stop taking action until you get there. Keep taking action. Never stop taking action! Before you get to the last chapter, think about the things in your life that don't feel right. By 'don't feel right', I mean things that cause you stress and anxiety. These are sure signs something isn't right. These are the things that need a healthy dose of action to create change.

I didn't change my situation overnight. But if I hadn't chosen to face my fears and create change, nothing would have changed. I would be stuck in an environment I hate – just because I didn't want to look like a failure in the eyes of others. Instead, I worked towards becoming more true to myself by doing more of the things that made me happy. That also involved not being afraid of what others *might* have thought about what I was doing. That led to a new situation with a lot less anxiety, stress, insecurity and illness. You are more than capable of doing the same in any situation you're not happy with! Try it and see.

Park your ego

There are a couple of things standing in the way of you being true to yourself. One is other people. But there is another significant contributing factor: *you.* Or, to be more specific, *your ego.* We're about to go to war with your ego. Your ego is your biggest obstacle when it comes to mental freedom.

There is a side of your ego that isn't all bad, however. That's the bit that can aid and boost your genuine confidence. It's the bit that can fuel your belief and get you taking action, even when the odds are against you. But there's also the other side. There aren't many good things to say about this side of your ego. This is the egotistical side that we're going to go to war with. It's this side that will have you doing all sorts of silly things. One of these things is confusing assertiveness with aggression. Do you know someone who thinks they are assertive, when really they're just aggressive (or passive-aggressive)?

I cringe when I see a party in a restaurant and the classic passive-aggressive character (because there is always one in a large group) clicks his finger to get the waiter's attention. As the waiter approaches the table, he speaks to him like he's a piece of dirt, ordering him to hurry up with his order of wine. He also complains a lot, even if the service and food are good. All of this bravado is an attempt to demonstrate his strength, driven by his ego and need to impress others. In other words, *his ego is in charge.*

Apart from aggressive public displays, the ego will dredge up all that's unpleasant in your personality. Your ego depends on external factors to make you feel confident and happy. It needs to be constantly fed, and when it's lacking attention, it will encourage you to do stupid things. You only need to look at social media to see the endless examples of what I'm talking about here. Half-naked selfies, trout pouts and fake smiles are just the start.

Unfortunately, we're breeding a society built on ego. Young people today are being led to believe that they need to look a certain way to feel good and be confident. This is rubbish – and it's all down to a lack of education. My hope is these kids get hold of this book so they can nip this egotistical behaviour in the bud, before they have a nervous breakdown about not fitting in. If somebody had told me from an early age that confidence comes from within, and not from what people on TV told me, I'd have achieved much more, much earlier – and I'd have been much happier and less socially anxious in the process.

Your ego is at its most dangerous when it needs to be right. And seeing as that's one of the fundamental needs of your ego, it's something you need to be very aware of.

The need to be right is a negative trait and not good for you. The ego clings on to this need to be right in such an extreme way that you'll hold on to old beliefs – beliefs that have been holding you back and keeping you trapped in social anxiety. Your ego will fight to make them right. Let me give you an example. If you hate confident people because you think they're arrogant, your ego will work against you becoming confident! Subconsciously, you will continue to view confidence as a bad thing. It's the same for any beliefs. If you've always hated rich and successful people, for example, your ego will fight to ensure you'll never be rich or successful! This sounds very counterproductive, maybe even a little crazy, but that's how the ego and subconscious work. Confidence, being rich and being successful could all be viewed as being superficial. But imagine what would happen if you started hating happy or clever people. Your ego and subconscious would work towards you never achieving these things. That's crazy.

Ditch the need to be right, and ditch your old beliefs while you're at it. They're holding you back. Use the *logical gap* (a technique we're about to cover) to help you appreciate when your ego is at play and when old negative beliefs are clouding your mind. The sure sign of both of these things is the need to react instantly and be right.

Say bye-bye to that ego, and you'll begin to experience too many benefits for me to list here. A rapid decrease in social anxiety is just one of them.

Emotion vs logic

Have you noticed; when you react emotionally to someone (or something), you tend to regret it later? Anger leads to fights. Sadness leads to doing something to fill your emotional hole – such as eating a pot of double-chocolate fudge ice cream. Envy makes you pull out your credit card and buy things to impress people you don't like. Fear leads to inaction.

We are led by our emotions.

Emotions are basically shortcut reactions to tell us how we feel about something (or someone). Sometimes these impulsive reactions serve us well, but most of the time they don't. When they don't serve us well, we buy things we don't need. TV shopping channels make healthy profits from these impulses. Look at the products they sell. They aren't necessities; they're impulse buys you tend to regret later. We start relationships with people who are no good for us – people who drain our emotions (toxic people). And we accept jobs that are not right for us – jobs that end up being blips on our CV.

TV adverts are a good example of how emotion dominates our actions and drives our impulsions. I mentioned TV ads at the start of the book, and how angry and frustrated I get when I watch them. With their high-pitched music, puppies and sad faces, they are designed to pull on every emotional string you have. Why? Because it's emotion that will get you up off the sofa and make you buy things – which is the advertising agency's only focus. Adverts don't mind making you angry, afraid, surprised or disgusted either. They'll take all those emotions, as well as sadness and happiness. Why?

Because *any* emotion is good. Indifference and logic are the advertising agency's enemies. Indifference means the advert hasn't worked. You are unmoved. Logic means you're self-aware and have control over your actions, including what you spend your money on. Logic has power, and we'll focus on it here.

Until we become more self-aware of our emotional reactions, we'll continue to be led by them. But logic will tip the balance in our favour. Let's put this theory into two categories.

Category 1: The head (logic).
Category 2: The heart (emotion).

Without category 2 (emotion), we couldn't function as humans. However, issues arise when we have too much heart. It's not nice, but we have to accept the fact the nicer you are, the more you may be taken advantage of. What are you willing to do? What do you view as acceptable? If you're a people-pleaser (and you will be if you care too much about what people think), there will be a queue forming in front of you of unscrupulous people waiting to take advantage. It's worth noting that these people can also include the people closest to us, like parents and friends.

As I mentioned earlier, I'm not suggesting that you stop being a decent, caring person. Just do it in a way that protects yourself from toxic people. Tip the balance using logic. I'm sure you've got your own examples of an imbalanced relationship, but I'm going to use the following example to list some traits of a toxic friend to give you an idea of what I'm talking about here.

Example

You have a close friend you've known for many years. She's not what you would call reliable. She makes it a habit to cancel on you at short notice, and when she does turn up, she's usually late. She doesn't stay long because she always has something else on, and when she talks, it's about her favourite subject (herself): *Oh, my day has been hectic. Work has been non-stop. My boss is on my back again. This coffee is cold. I might have a cake. Liam is getting into trouble at school again....* It's unlikely the conversation will ever be about you.

The conversations you have with her are just one small example of the lack of balance in your friendship. You are the one who always forgives and forgets, but when it comes to something you do or say, it's a different story. You're prepared to be open and honest (because you know that's what makes a good relationship), but you won't get that same level of honesty or openness back. Your friend will happily moan at you, but she would rather live a lie than say how miserable her life really is. Your friendship is one-sided, and her life is always better than yours. It makes her feel better to have one up on you. For example, if things are challenging in your relationship, hers will be perfect. She'll say, 'Oh, poor you. Things at home have never been better for me. It's like we're going through our honeymoon all over again!' (Even if that's not true.)

In this example, *emotion* will tell you that you've been friends for a long time, and she's always been like this. When she says something nasty, she didn't really mean it. You should just put up with it. Just like you should ignore her one-upmanship and her lack of honesty. All this is a stark contrast to what logic will be telling you. *Logic* will get you asking questions like 'What am I doing wasting my precious time on someone who drains me? What am I getting from this relationship? I've known her a long time, but that doesn't mean I have to sacrifice my own happiness to stay loyal. Do I need to keep meeting up with her every week? I've got better things to be doing!'

Doesn't logic sound great?

The outcome we want in any scenario is a good balance between emotion and logic.

If you balance emotion and logic in this example, you'll realise that meeting this person isn't worth your time (logic). Your heart (emotion) will tell you that you don't need to hurt your friend's feelings, so the happy balance might be to not see them as often, until you feel comfortable with not seeing them any more (logic). You'll continue to feel guilty about it (emotion), but your happiness and well-being will improve, helping you to see you made the right decision after all (logic).

In more extreme circumstances, such as when physical abuse is part of the behaviour, immediately detaching yourself from the person is a logical approach. Nobody deserves any form of abuse, especially physical. Don't stay in a relationship that is bad for you and don't feel you have to keep pleasing everyone else by sacrificing your own happiness and safety.

Using a combination of emotion and logic is a powerful skill to have.

It's difficult to get right, but your common sense will help – it will tell you when you're using too much emotion or logic. Feedback will come to you when you're feeling excessive guilt, anxiety, anger or sadness, or when you're being colder than is necessary. Watch and listen to all feedback, and use it to get the balance right.

A logical gap

By giving yourself a gap between the *emotion* you experience and the *action* you take, you'll transform the way you deal with any situation, including the way you feel towards it. This is all about self-control, and not letting your ego or pride dictate who you are. I call this exercise the 'logical gap'.

You can use this technique in any situation or circumstance. You can use it to stop an argument. Use it so an argument doesn't begin in the first place. Use it to improve relationships. Use it in business meetings and when managing people. Use it to get your kids to bed. Any time, anywhere, any place – it will work effectively however and wherever you use it.

Have you noticed how James Bond only reacts when he needs to? You'll see him jumping off a building to catch a baddy and dodging bullets, but when it's not a life-or-death situation, he's calm, relaxed and in control. Bond uses logic as much as emotion, which is why he's got bags of self-control.

If someone pisses you off today, it will be your emotion, not your logic, that will keep you feeling pissed off. It's emotion that will keep you trapped in thoughts of anger and resentment. It's logic that will help you break free from it.

Being led by emotion generally leads to actions you will regret. People fight and argue because both parties are being driven by emotion (anger). If logic were to kick in for one of these people, it would tell them that having a shouting match in the middle of their son's birthday party serves little purpose – especially for the birthday boy, who is crying in the corner of the room. Emotion (anger, in this instance) fuels the shouting match. Logic douses the anger by helping the individual see how pointless arguing in this fashion is.

As part of your new 'can't care' mentality, I want you to get in the habit of using more logic. We're going to achieve that by creating a *logical gap* between your emotion and your reaction (action). For example, if someone says something to you that makes you instantly angry, you will use your logical gap so you don't react straightaway. You don't need to. It's your ego and emotion that are telling you to react straightaway, and that's when you lose all your power. Think about it. If someone says something to you that makes you instantly angry, they want that reaction. That's their intention. If you react, you're playing straight into their hands. They've won.

It might feel good at the time to react to an insult with a punch, but where does it get us? Our strength lies is in the logic of not reacting. Our pride and need to react keep us weak. True strength lies in not getting tangled in their web of toxicity.

Emotion tends to override logic, but the true power is in the logic.

When we create a logical gap between emotion and action, we don't have shouting matches with people who want to keep us trapped in their negativity. We don't fight – unless it's needed as a defence. And we don't sit rocking back and forth, worrying about what other people *might* be thinking, because logic tells us it's stupid to do so. (Please note: An instant reaction is good when a fist is heading towards your face. In this instance, an instant reaction in the form of a dodge is highly logical!)

People will say and do something to you because they're looking for a reaction. When we get sucked into negativity, we're giving away our power. No power means you're weak, and when you're weak, you get taken advantage of. (A cruel fact of life.) Weakness is as much about suffering as it is being taken advantage of.

Like all effective power, it's better held within ourselves, distributed at a time to suit us, not when it suits everyone else. Don't expend your energy to suit others. Keep your energy to make you stronger, and use it when you choose to use it. Use it when someone comes along and tries to snare you in their negative web – use the logical gap to spot it before they get a chance.

We're not robots, so creating a logical gap can be tricky, especially when someone makes you angry. It does get easier the more you do it. Just keep your ego and pride in check –

they will encourage you to react quickly with emotion. To help, I count, and that might be useful for you as well. For example, if someone says something to me that I would usually react angrily to, I'll mentally count from 1, 2, 3... until I'm back in a place of logic. The more I've done this, the quicker I've got. I can now get back to a place of logic in under a count of five. It's because I've programmed my brain to associate counting with logic. As soon as I start counting, my brain knows to switch from emotion to logic. By the time I've got to five, the need to lash out has gone, and the person looking to entwine me in their web of negativity has well and truly lost.

Get in the habit of creating a logical gap, and use counting if it helps. To begin with, you might find you have to count past ten. That doesn't matter. There is no magic number. It depends heavily on the situation, the person, and what's been said. In some circumstances, you might have to count for some time. I know I have. You may even need to walk away. All of this is fine. You're listening to yourself and becoming more self-aware, including learning what suits you best. You're not allowing your environment, including other people, to dictate your mood or actions. You'll quickly come to discover that doing what is right for you is where the power lies.

With time, you'll get better and quicker at using your logic, and the gap will get shorter. You'll be able to have free-flowing conversations while training yourself to use your logic as much as your emotion. If your delayed response annoys someone, that is their problem, not yours. You can't care about that. If the conversation is worth having, they'll wait. If they wanted an instant reaction from you, it's highly likely their intention was to wind you up anyway. By not reacting as they wanted, you're in control.

When you get yourself in the habit of not responding instantly, you will be a master communicator. Your self-control will improve and you will take big strides towards freeing yourself from social anxiety. If you want the ability to dictate your mood, including reducing your anxiety in public, self-control is a crucial piece of the puzzle.

Remember, the aim here isn't to become a robot with no emotion. Emotion isn't bad. Emotion makes us human and different from robots. It's just that we tend not to use logic when we need to, so this exercise will be good for most of us. Adding a sprinkle more logic to your life could make all the difference.

Voices tell lies

When that voice in your head tells you something, you have to remember that that voice is based on habit, conditioning and ego. It's not always right. In fact, it's some of the worst advice you might get! I know how crazy this sounds, believe me. But it's important to remember: the voice in your head isn't always the best thing to listen to.

This voice is based primarily on your *survival*. It's this survival-type way of thinking that can turn a good time bad, within the time it takes to think the thought. For example, you're invited to a party, then your voice kicks in with all the what ifs. *What if this... What if that...* The good time you were going to have at the party has been destroyed because your voice has come up with one hundred different ways you'll die on your way there. By the time you've spent three weeks worrying about it all and overthinking it, you've locked yourself in your bedroom to protect yourself against your own thoughts.

Think about your inner voice like this. Imagine you had a friend who only thought about surviving. Being around him would seriously get to you after a while, wouldn't it? It wouldn't be long before you quickly and politely declined his birthday party invitations. He would be incredibly dull, very anal, depressing and deadly boring! (Maybe you have a friend like this already?) Replace this friend with the voice in your head, because when you pay attention, they sound very similar.

Don't ask her out. She'll never say yes and you'll look like a fool when she laughs at you.

Don't ask for that pay rise, you haven't worked hard enough to deserve it. The boss is only going to say no.

Don't laugh at your own joke. You might think it's funny but no one else is laughing. You'll embarrassed yourself again, you fool.

Sound familiar?

There is no one more effective at beating you up than that voice in your head. There is no person more skilled at stopping you from trying something new. That voice in your head is stunting your growth. It has a unique ability to create all sorts of problems – things that don't exist. The voice creates stories and catastrophises to the point where we give up before we even start. It makes things seem a whole lot worse than they actually are.

That voice is the result of years (depending how old you are) of conditioning via endless sources. Parents. TV. Teachers. Friends. Advertising. The voice is telling you to react based on survival and habit. A lot of these habits are based on false beliefs – beliefs you've lived by for years that you don't bother to question because they are simply your reality. These beliefs might have served you when you were a kid, but they don't today.

If you regress a little again, a lot of the negative thoughts you have will be based on fears you had as a kid. Do you ever feel like a child – unsafe, vulnerable and unprotected? Now you're a responsible adult. You have options and choices. This is precisely why that voice isn't always right. It should be questioned – particularly when you feel you're not getting the result you want. Or when you feel like giving up. Or when your ego is leading your actions. The more you practise questioning the voice in your head, the more self-aware you become, and the more control you gain over your feelings and actions, including how you feel socially.

But let's be fair. The voice is your head isn't all bad. It gets things right as well. We can't be battling ourselves 24/7. You've got to get the balance right and be able to put trust in yourself and your instincts. Do that. Trust yourself and your instincts – that's important. You've worked hard to develop your intuitive skills. Just start paying attention to the voice when it's holding you back.

The next time that voice pipes up and tells you that you can't do something, ask, 'Why not? Go ahead and provide me with proof that I'll fail.' Treat it with the contempt it deserves – just like you would if it were someone else continually putting you down and ripping you apart.

Unlike a third party, who you don't have control over, you *do* have control over your inner voice. With self-awareness, you can retrain your inner voice to give you inspiration and motivation when you need it, rather than put you down. When you continue to question, you'll develop new thinking patterns that aid your growth and development. Your inner voice will start working with you, rather than against you.

When someone puts you down or tries to make you feel inadequate, your inner voice will be strong enough to fend off any negativity that could arise from that. It will protect and guard, and won't add to the negativity. That's a great mental position to be in.

Comfort over conformity

A friend recently had surgery on her excruciating bunions. The cause: wearing high-heeled shoes for over twenty years!

My question after her op was simple: *Was it worth it?* She thought about the answer for a few seconds as she looked down at her bandages. I was shocked that her immediate answer wasn't 'God, no!' It puzzled me that the excruciating pain and her deformed feet didn't make her full of regret and resentment. How could wearing high-heeled shoes with the intention to impress other people have been worth it? She argued that it wasn't just about impressing other people. She wore them to feel confident. To feel powerful. To make a statement. I asked, 'Aren't these things the same as wanting to impress other people?' She eventually agreed that the high heels could have been a mistake when she got up to walk to the kitchen, her face scrunched and full of pain.

Where are the bunions in your life?

What are you doing that is causing long-term pain and irreparable discomfort for the sake of impressing others? Whatever it is, it's not worth it. It's just fuelling your social anxiety.

What does 'comfort over conformity' mean? Some people might ask why I drive a BMW instead of a Hyundai. Hyundais are cheaper, and they get you from A to B, just like a BMW. I have nothing against Hyundais – but, like any other cheaper brand of car, they don't have the same level of quality or comfort that a BMW provides. To me, this isn't snobbery; it's wanting a little more quality and comfort. To get that quality and comfort, it means I usually have to spend a little more money to get it. (If I can afford it, and it's worth it.) For example, I wouldn't buy a cheap pair of trainers, because most cheap trainers are poor quality. The fact that trainers have ticks or stripes on them is insignificant if they're comfortable and good quality, meaning they'll last. If I bought trainers for their ticks and stripes, that would be me trying to keep up with those Joneses again.

If everyone is buying something, like a gadget or fashion item, but you think it's terrible, don't buy it. 'Everyone' is rarely right. Take your sheep head off and make your own choices based on your own preferences. Do what makes *you* feel happy and content. Buy something because you like it. Don't be sucked in by trends and by what everyone else is doing. If you do, you're conforming with the masses – the same people who rarely get it right.

End the chase

I mentioned 'emotional holes' earlier. They are metaphorical holes within ourselves that we try to fill to deal with our misery and discontent. We fill them with clothes, jewellery, cars, make-up or one-night stands. The trouble with all these things is that they are temporary fixes to long-term social anxiety issues. The reason is simple: *when you don't deal with the root cause of your discontent, you can't fix it.* No material possession in the world will help. No cosmetic procedure. No sexual desire fulfilled. The emotional hole will remain and you'll keep looking for the next fix. Filling the emotional hole for the long term and dealing with social anxiety requires us to understand the chase.

Have you noticed that the things you go chasing after end up owning you? The expensive car gets you into debt. Your ambition to become a millionaire puts you in hospital with mental and physical health issues. You finally get a date with someone you've fancied for ages, only for her to drop you like a hot potato, leaving you emotionally battered and bruised. Her expectations of where you were going to eat and what car you'd be driving should have been clues that you were chasing the wrong person.

When you can't care, you don't chase things not worth chasing.

I'm not suggesting money, possessions, relationships or anything worth having just come to you – you and I both know they don't. Most of us have to work for the things that are worth having. The trick is making the work as enjoyable as the goal. In other words, make the journey as enjoyable and worthwhile as the destination. This is easier said than done, but when you become more aware of the need to do it, you can start to improve the only thing that counts – this moment, right now.

Get rich or die tryin' is literal. Is it worth your while making a $1 million only to end up having a heart attack? Your health is everything. What is the point of money if you don't have your health? The same goes for getting into debt and chasing after people who aren't really interested.

What are you chasing right now?

It seems inherent in us humans to want more. No matter how much we achieve, it's never enough. We're also good at wanting things we can't have. Get instant satisfaction and reduce your social anxiety by ending the chase. If it is meant to be, it will be. Work towards your goals and take action to make them happen. Just don't do it at the expense of your well-being and health.

Instead, refocus on what matters. What matters can usually be counted on one hand. You, your health, the way you feel, the people closest to you are all that matter. This realisation normally hits people on their deathbed, or when they miss the opportunity to say goodbye to a loved one. Don't wait that long. Let this serve as your wake-up call.

Aim to serve rather than consume and chase. Serving others is the best and most effective way of ending the chase – and of filling your emotional hole and finding true fulfilment. By serving, you might also find that the things you've been chasing come as a healthy by-product of giving and achieving. If they do, you'll enjoy them much more than if you have to chase them. Take money, for example. If you set up a business with the intention of serving others, rather than getting rich, you might find the journey between the two very different. Set up the business to serve and money becomes a healthy by-product of that. Set up the business to get rich, and you'll stay trapped chasing something that has no substance, meaning or end goal. Serving others is all that counts, because when you do that, you serve yourself.

Serving others could be something as small as giving up an hour of your time a week to volunteer, to something as big as adopting or fostering. Start by asking yourself, 'What can I do to stop chasing and consuming as much as I am, and instead aim to give and serve?' When I asked myself that question, that started a whole new way of thinking and life for me – one with a lot less social anxiety.

One of our biggest mistakes is believing that, the more we own and the more flashy stuff we've got, like sports cars, watches, designer clothes, handbags, shoes and big houses, the more people will like and respect us. When was the last time you liked someone who raced past you in a vehicle that cost more than your house? Expensive possessions won't get you more friends. If they do, they won't be real friends.

Buying things with the sole purpose of impressing others is the trap. The more we own, the more the anxiety and stress mount up. A lot of mental freedom comes from detachment and simplicity. Consider if you need all the things you own. Have a good clear-out of unwanted stuff. Doesn't it feel great? There is something cathartic about having a good clear-out. Start with your wardrobe. When did you last look through your clothes to check the ones you haven't worn for a year? They're just taking up space (mental and physical). Get 'em gone! I used to have about ten pairs of jeans. I now have two. When I looked at them all, those two pairs were the only ones I wore. The rest just took up space and, worse than that, put debt on the credit card that added to my anxiety.

Bad debt vs good debt

The need for possessions gets us into bad debt. This is the type of debt that serves no purpose. A good example is taking out a loan to buy a car you can't afford. Nowadays, car companies make it extra-easy to get into bad debt with things like personal contract purchase agreements. These finance deals are attractive because you don't have to put much money down at the start. Instead, they sting you at the end when it's time to change your car. These agreements are the reason you see a lot of your neighbours driving expensive German cars while their kids look malnourished.

Bad debt is a $8,000 credit card debt racked up on possessions that are now worth zero – possessions you've hardly used and can't remember. Things like eight pairs of jeans at the bottom of your wardrobe. (Including six pairs you've never worn, with the tags still on them.)

Good debt is the type of debt that gives you a return. For example, investing in educating yourself, such as doing a college course or evening class. If that education leads to you enhancing your career or starting your own business, that's a positive return on your investment. Borrowing money from the bank to purchase something that gives you a monthly return, like a buy-to-let house, is good debt because you get a return on your investment (as long as you can afford repayments).

Good debt is a 0% credit card with no fee you use to increase your credit score when you need to – like when applying for a buy-to-let mortgage. You pay the balance off each month in full. As an extra bonus, unlike a debit card, using a credit card also protects you against fraud. (If you spend on your debit card and you're subject to fraud, your bank doesn't cover you. It's your loss. When it happens on your credit card, you're fully covered. Handy!)

For the love of God, focus on good debt. Bad debt will get you nowhere, fast. Bad debt is the reason I had a £50,000 debt with nothing to show for it, and the reason the average household has about the same. Bad debt will keep you trapped and anxious. It will have you dreading the postman knocking on the door each day, and the sound of final reminders hitting your mat. It will make sure that you retire no earlier than the government tells you – usually about five years before you die from exhaustion.

As I say above, debt, used to your advantage, can be positive. But I'm not a financial advisor, and this isn't a book on financial advice. The book I recommend on the subject of finance is *Rich Dad Poor Dad* by Robert T. Kiyosaki. It's one of my favourite books. Money will always be one of our biggest anxieties and stresses. The ability to worry less about money is life-changing. That's why I've included this section in this book. Finding out how to handle money leads to more self-awareness and knowledge about it, including financial changes you can make that will make the difference for you. Spending less on unnecessary purchases to impress others is a big change you can make. To find out more, read more about it and get financially educated.

Be a maverick

I've always had massive respect for anyone who has had the courage to do something on their own terms – especially when it goes against what everyone else is doing and everything they're been told they 'should' do.

Going against the crowd is not easy. It goes against our instincts and our innate need for approval (the feelings we get that tell us to fall back in line whenever we might be strolling too far away from the herd). A good example of someone defying the odds and going against the crowd is Seth Godin. I read Seth's blog every day. It's one of the most popular blogs in the world, and it's completely different to anything else you will see. Most blogs are lengthy and detailed, and if you subscribe to them, you'll likely get them about once a week. Seth's blog is sent out *every day*. They're usually a couple of paragraphs long, but sometimes they're only one sentence long. Who would have thought that would work? Seth could easily have conformed to the idea that you have to produce lots of content to get top rankings on Google. But by running his own race, he produced one of the world's most read and unique blogs. Seth has a 'can't care' mentality.

People like Seth have taught me to run my own race. It's a concept that, over the years, I've struggled with. I wouldn't describe myself as a natural maverick. I blame a lot of that on the anxiety I went through for years – it tends to put you in your place. But I've worked on my maverick qualities and got better at doing more of the things I want to do because I want to do them that way. And boy, is my life better for it! I won't just do something because everyone else is doing it. When you can adopt a maverick-type mentality, it will change the way you think and feel.

Don't just go with everyone else. Conform when you have to, like having to work to keep the roof over your head, but do it while developing your maverick skills. Get some more balance in your life by doing more of the things you *want* to do. If you're working 9–5, what maverick qualities can you develop to balance that out? Could you get a side hustle, for example? (I won't go into detail about what side hustles are. It's a big subject, with books written about it. If you want to know more, Google 'passive income' – that will get you started.)

Even when it goes against the norm, if it feels right to you, then it is right. All that matters is how you feel.

The 9–5 felt very wrong to me from a young age. I knew I had to do something to change it, even when everyone else just got on with it. What's the point of doing something if you hate doing it, or it doesn't feel right? Yes, we all have to do things we don't want to do (like the job I just mentioned), but we can aim to get a better balance if we choose to. You can take the small steps needed to create the big changes you want – everyone is capable of that. These changes might not happen overnight, but they'll *never* happen unless you take action. When you feel like something is impossible to do, it's worthwhile looking around. Who has already done what you want to do? How did they do it? That should give you extra motivation and belief to make it happen.

Our greatest fulfilment comes from doing what we *want* to do – what feels right to us. I'm not necessarily talking about success in relation to money (something we tend to gauge success on). If you're doing what you feel is right, you achieve contentment and self-satisfaction. If money comes with that, great, that's a nice bonus.

Why do you think so many millionaires are unhappy, even after they've achieved all the financial goals they thought they wanted to achieve? It's because they looked at things backwards. They thought that money was the route to happiness, rather than happiness being the route to money. Wouldn't you rather have fun on your journey, be a maverick and do what is right for you, than chase a goal that makes you do things you're not happy about – especially when you reach the goal only to discover it doesn't make you happy?

Being a maverick and doing what is right for you might not be for everyone. There is no doubt that you'll get raised eyebrows along the way. But who cares? You can't care. Do what feels right to you. All the pioneers of the world had to do something different to create something special and unique. If they followed the crowd and did what everyone else was doing, they would produce the same results as everyone else.

Without mavericks like Seth, Elon and Steve, the world would stagnate. (I bet you knew who I was referring to just from their first names. Doesn't that just prove what you have to do to stand out and be extraordinary? There are 400,000+ Steves in the USA alone!) OK, you might not have ambitions to revolutionise technology like Steve Jobs, but feeling good about yourself starts at home. It begins and ends in your mind. Who knows, when you start being more true to yourself, where that might take you? What possibilities could be available to you when you drop the need to follow everyone else? I don't know for sure, but I do know it will rapidly decrease your social anxiety.

Run your own race

Would you run a serious 100-metre race against Usain Bolt? Would you get in the ring with Ali in his prime? Would you pit yourself against Whitney in a karaoke comp? You wouldn't do any of these things because Bolt would make you look like an OAP on the track. Ali would knock your head clean off. And even though you gave all the high notes of 'I Will Always Love You' a good go, Whitney would have wrecked the mic! These people are all fantastic at what they do. Here I've used them to highlight the stupidity of competing against others when it's not called for. In most circumstances, pitting yourself against others isn't necessary.

Would you like to know the quickest route to becoming socially anxious?

Comparing yourself to others.

We compare ourselves to others all day, every day – mostly to our deep dissatisfaction. We pit ourselves against family, friends, colleagues, bosses, spouses, kids, neighbours – you name it. The person walking down the road is looking at the guy riding the bike, the guy riding the bike is looking at the guy in the car, the guy in the car is looking at the guy in the newer, flashier sports car, and the guy in the sports car is looking above him at the guy in the helicopter. And the cycle of dissatisfaction and lack of gratitude continues! When do we stop comparing ourselves against others and find gratitude for what we already have?

I'm not suggesting you never enter a competition again, or forget about being the best salesperson in your office. I'm talking about everyday life. Stop running a race against people in *everything* you do. Focus on yourself. Focus on where you are and where you want to be. That's the only thing that's important.

If your friend wants to be the next big business owner, and you're happy and content working for a charity, so be it. Be happy for your friend, as you want them to be happy for you. Don't let social and peer pressure steer you in a direction you don't want to go. Only you know what's right for you. Feeling social anxiety is a sure sign things aren't right.

The more you compare your life to others, the more miserable you will be. Nothing will ever be enough. There will always be someone smarter than you. Someone more attractive than you. Someone more athletic than you. Get over it. Be OK with it.

You're unique. You also possess qualities that others envy!

Never forget your core

No matter how you choose to move forward from this point, including how much you might like to change or be like your favourite celeb or actress, you can only change a certain amount. **This is a significant message**, so I want you to pay attention. It really is the difference between you finding joy and living a miserable life, full of social anxiety.

There has been a sudden rush of people talking about the benefits of getting up at 5am. I did a bit of research, and I must admit, I liked what I read. I decided to give it a go – even though I am not what you would class a 'morning person'. I'm being polite. I hate getting out of my pit! Who doesn't? The advice I read told me not to worry about that – loads of people aren't morning people and make it work. With a little apprehension, I dutifully set my alarm for 5am the next day.

My alarm went off. It felt like it had only been five minutes since my head had hit the pillow. I was knackered and red-eyed. My pit was lovely and warm. *Nah!* I hit the snooze button and when the alarm sounded again a few minutes later, I switched it off and went back to sleep. I woke up naturally at my usual time of 7am – not knackered and not red-eyed.

Although 5am felt like an ungodly hour, I was disappointed in myself. I felt like I'd let myself down. *What a fat lazy stinking pile of crap you are*, I thought. (There is no one who will beat you up more than yourself!) The next morning I was determined to make it happen and not let the snooze button beat me. I went to bed a little earlier, set my alarm for 5am, and I did it! I got up at 5am, did a bit of work for an hour, hit the gym at 6am, showered and had breakfast, all before 8am. Wow! I got so much more done. *This new lifestyle is amazing,* I thought. *I can see what all the fuss is about.* But wait. There was one big problem. I hated it! I gave it a good go and followed the routine for over a week, but I absolutely despised it. I got loads more done before 8am, but I was tired, grumpy, and felt like I'd aged thirty years in one week. Not just because of how I felt physically and mentally, but because I was ready for lunch at 10am, dinner at 3pm, and bed at 7pm. I was the only person under the age of sixty-five enjoying the early bird specials!

I gave it longer than a week to make sure my decision not to continue with it was the right one, and it just didn't work for me. I enjoy working in the evening. I have more energy later in the day. I like to get up when I feel like it. Don't get me wrong, OAPs are great company, but I like my dinner at 6pm. That is the core of who I am. If not getting up at 5am makes me lazy and unmotivated, so be it. I accept that I have faults. I accept that I'm not perfect. I'm OK with the fact that others might think and feel differently to me. I'm being true to myself and sticking with my core.

What makes you, you? What makes up your core?

Take some time to think about this. What's important to you? What things might you be doing that are going against the core of who you are? Are you doing these things because everyone else is doing them? Are those skinny jeans *really* that comfortable? How about those six-inch stilettos? Are they worth the bunions? The suit? The hair? The jewellery? The attitude? You get the picture.

Start being true to yourself and get back to the core of who you are. Develop your 'can't care' mentality by being comfortable with your uniqueness. When you work with the core of what makes you unique, the world is a better, less anxious place to live in.

Are you embarrassed?

What is embarrassment, anyway? Think of what embarrassment means to you for a second. Think of how you feel when you're embarrassed. It's all made up by you, isn't it? It's that feeling you get when you've done something you think makes you look stupid – it's a feeling created by you. If you didn't think what you'd done was stupid, you wouldn't be embarrassed, even if the other ten people in the room thought it was embarrassing. In other words, embarrassment is all about perception. And, like anything we perceive, we can change our view about it.

You've probably met some people who do and say outrageous things and act like it's normal? They'll say something shameful and shocking, and you'll look at them, expecting them to go red. But it doesn't happen. Embarrassment is not on their agenda. Like the guy who wears a bright Hawaiian shirt to work and is happy to tell everyone about the sexual nightmare he had last night. (And by everyone, I mean *everyone*!) Compare him to someone who's self-conscious about pretty much everything they do and say, who regularly blushes, and the mental difference is vast. Their embarrassment threshold is very different.

I used to suffer terribly from being red-faced. Any form of attention would bring it on. I used to dread a conversation or social situation in case someone turned around and said, 'Carl, what do you think?' Boom – instant red face! 'Er, wh-wh-what? Me? Er, no. I mean, I don't know. What did you say again?' While stumbling over my words, I'd hope the conversation and attention would move past me as if I was invisible.

Feeling that you want the floor to swallow you up in public is horrible. It's the worst. No one should have the displeasure of suffering it. We'll all have embarrassing moments, for sure, but feeling constantly shy is no fun. There is a better balance to be had, and we get that better balance by first appreciating what embarrassment is: *nothing more than a feeling we create from a thought or belief we have*. When you look it at it like this, you expose it and take away its potential power.

Embarrassment wouldn't exist if other people didn't exist, would it? If you tripped over the corner of a rug, what would it matter if nobody were around to see it? Nobody would be there to laugh at you. Your cheeks would stay the same colour. You'd laugh it off, and maybe give the rug a damn good telling-off. (Again, with no one to judge your sanity.)

Compare this to tripping on a rug in a crowded hotel lobby. How much more likely are you to be embarrassed and red-faced?

Why do we feel embarrassed when people are watching us, and how can we overcome it?

There's a lot of biological and psychological reasons behind getting embarrassed. If you want to know all the science, there are plenty of books out there on it. I'm not going to bore you with that. Instead, we'll get straight to the solution, and these four things will help you overcome embarrassment:

1. The ability to feel comfortable with being judged
If you're going to get past feelings of embarrassment, you have to be comfortable with being judged. Easier said than done, I know, so here's how you do it. Ask yourself, 'What's the worst that can happen from being judged?' The last time I checked, the worst that can come from being judged is having somebody talk badly about you. That's about as bad as it gets.

If you fear being judged, my advice is to do nothing, say nothing, and be nothing. If you want to achieve things in your life, being judged is always going to be part of the process. It's time you started getting comfortable with that fact.

Turn being judged around from a negative and see it as a positive. When people are judging you, at least they're paying attention. They want to give you their opinion. In other words, *you matter*. Surely that has to be better than being insignificant, even if it does come with adverse judgement at times?

2. The ability to laugh at yourself

Being Mr Serious never got anybody anywhere. Sorry, that's a lie. It gets you a one-way ticket to Analville, where embarrassment is common. Here, everybody takes everything they do so seriously that they forget to see the funny side of life. Smiles are non-existent. Frowns, raised shoulders, stiff necks and clenched fists are the standard look in Analville.

I lived in Analville for some time. I only appreciated how bad a place it was when I escaped it. I managed to get out of it by developing the ability to laugh at myself. Not being perfect used to cause me great social anxiety. Now it makes me chuckle.

Every now and again I go back to Analville (everybody slips into old habits), but looking at all the misery caused by the seriousness reminds me what a crap place it is. Now, when I find myself there, I leave in a hurry and take my sense of humour with me.

Have you taken a trip to Analville recently? Maybe you live there. Perhaps you visit frequently. Skip the embarrassment, ditch the seriousness, and stay away. Use your sense of humour, even if you have to dig deep for it, and keep seeing the funny side of every situation, insecurity and imperfection. If you're struggling with a particular insecurity, physical or mental, make a joke of it. If you're really struggling, watch your favourite comedian, who will remind of you how to do it. Ricky Gervais is my go-to guy. If you follow Ricky on Twitter, you'll see that he makes jokes about how fat he is, with pictures of himself in the bath squeezing his man boobs together. A good example of what I'm talking about here.

When you can laugh at yourself, nobody can laugh at you. Nobody can make you feel small about an insecurity or imperfection if you're laughing at it. If anything, it makes the person trying look stupid.

3. The ability to see everybody as human

Respect and admiration for people who achieve big things is normal. An athlete, actor, musician, artist, writer – whoever your idols are, it's nice to have people to look up to. Mentors can show us the way. Even so, it's important to remember that these people are still people. They are human, just like you and me.

Today, we put celebrities on a pedestal. There are people who are famous for being famous – reality TV celebrities, for example. It's an issue. Why? Because it's not healthy. It distorts our view of what really counts in life, including actually achieving something of substance. It makes perfect sense to mimic the style of your favourite artist. You might want to re-create their genius strokes to make a similar piece of art. Copying the hairstyle of your favourite reality TV star doesn't quite have the same substance. Why is substance important? Because without it, there is nothing but fakery and pretence. That equals bags of social anxiety.

Not long ago, I was speaking at an event. I saw a kid start to cry because he got to speak to one of these reality TV celebrities I'm talking about. That kid is growing up to believe that you should idolise someone just because they've been on TV. His parents would be doing him a much better service if they told him to look up to people who have achieved something that is worth aspiring to. People like Einstein, Edison and Tesla. These people dedicated their lives to improving ours, rather than spending their time queueing up to get on reality TV shows. People (of all ages) think they just need to get on TV and they've 'made it'. But nothing could be further from the truth.

You can kind of understand why fans of Michael Jackson sobbed uncontrollably after they'd given him a hug. That dude was seriously talented. But Michael, like anyone else, was still human. That's the reality check that we all need. We sometimes forget that we're all human. We all make mistakes, and we all feel embarrassed at times – celebrities and idols included. We all sing out of tune at times. We've all tripped over a rug at some point. We've all said something silly and out of character to someone we fancy. When we realise we're not the only ones who feel the way we do, we stop singling ourselves out as dummies. We stop putting people on a pedestal and, in turn, worry a lot less about what they might think of us.

4. The ability to step forward

Keeping your opinions to yourself is called for on occasion – mainly for politeness – but if you're not prepared to step forward and tell people what's on your mind, you'll build the habit of insecurity and embarrassment rather than self-confidence and self-assurance. This means you'll consistently put yourself in a place of weakness. You'll be known as the person who keeps quiet, the one who just accepts the opinions of people who are prepared to step forward. You will be seen as a shrinking violet whose life is dictated by others.

Silence and reflection are fine, but only to a point. Introverts should command as much respect as extroverts. But if you're consistently silent, nobody will know what you're thinking and your reputation as being meek will precede you. Take as much thinking time as you need, but be prepared to communicate – be prepared to speak out and step forward. Authentic confidence requires that you speak out. If you don't, not only will your voice never be heard, but you'll also be developing the habit of insecurity and embarrassment. You'll get so good at it, everyone will recognise you for it. If you're fed up with being identified as that person, the only way to rectify that is to start speaking out. The more you do it, the more comfortable it will feel.

How do I look?

Did you know that mirrors are a relatively new invention? They were invented in Germany in the nineteenth century. Before then, if you wanted to know what you looked like, you'd have to get a dim view via a bit of polished metal, look at your reflection in some calm water, or depend on someone else to tell you. But today, how important do you think mirrors are in society? Would you be as self-conscious about how you looked if you couldn't easily and conveniently check yourself in the mirror every few minutes? It's worse today because you don't need a mirror at all. You can find out how you look by reaching into your pocket and grabbing your phone. Self-consciousness and insecurity are at your fingertips.

Can you imagine how quickly the personal care and beauty industry would collapse if all of a sudden no one cared about how they looked? Make-up companies, cream and oil companies, hair product companies – all of them, out of business, overnight. You only need to pop to your nearest department store to see how far away we are from that happening.

Although I hate to say it, these companies have nothing to fear, because we will always care about our appearance, and they know it. In fact, they know it so well that they like to keep reinforcing the fact with adverts, billboards, magazines and ads. They might as well write in big letters: 'BUY OUR PRODUCT OR YOU WILL BE UGLY AND NOBODY WILL LIKE YOU.'

However, we can make a difference. If I can get you thinking a little differently about appearance, then I've done a good job. This will get you taking great strides towards freeing yourself from social anxiety.

Beauty starts in your head. Not in the mirror.

You control how you feel, including how you feel about the way you look. Remember that the next time you get anxious about your appearance. By all means, dress up, look smart, and feel good about yourself. But do it for the right reasons. The 'right reasons' are based on how *you* feel. The 'wrong reasons' are for anything outside that, including insecurity and dressing up to impress everyone else.

Let's use common sense here. Nobody is going to buy from you or go near you if you haven't showered for two weeks. If that is a problem in your life, hit the shower and put on something appropriate. Very few of us are privileged enough not to have to work for a living. That means that most of us need to make sacrifices. That sacrifice could mean putting on a suit to go to work from Monday to Friday. If you really don't want to do that, you'll find a way to stop having to do it. But while you have no other choice, do what you've got to do – for the right reasons.

Maybe you enjoy wearing a suit? Maybe it makes you feel good? I'm glad. As a long as you're doing it for the right reasons. Do you need the suit to make you feel good? Does it give you the status you crave? That's a bit like needing someone else in your life to make it complete. When they're gone, what are you gonna do? When your life is built on this type of weak foundation with little substance, you're heading for a fall.

It's not how you look that matters, it's how you feel.

Have you ever been in a room and someone with a big presence, a certain type of energy, has walked in? What happens to the atmosphere? The person doesn't have to be devilishly handsome or stunningly beautiful. Looks only go so far when it comes to authentic confidence. I'm talking about *persona*. (It could also be looked at as *charisma*.) Some people just ooze confidence and persona, don't they? It doesn't matter what they look like. They have a glow about them, almost like an invisible aura, or energy. This type of social confidence comes from the inside and is reflected outward. In other words, how you perceive yourself internally will reflect who you are externally – no matter what you look like.

When you develop social confidence with your new 'can't care' mentality, you will become the person I'm talking about here. You will walk into a room and people will pay attention. They might even stop to look at you. I can guarantee they'll want to know more about you. They will naturally gravitate towards you, and the usual social awkwardness that comes with meeting new people will not be found. You might not want to be the centre of attention – that's fine. But may I suggest that this scenario is better than having no significance at all? It's also better than being crippled by social anxiety.

Because we live in such a superficial world where we're led to believe that looks are everything, I'll reinforce the point about looks again.

Social confidence has very little to do with what you look like.

Think of somebody you know who is socially confident. Maybe it's somebody close to you? Maybe it's an actor or actress? I can think of very confident actors and actresses who are not what you would call traditionally or conventionally attractive, yet they have hordes of fans lusting after them. It's rare you'll find these actors and actresses looking in the mirror wondering why God didn't give them better looks. They're too busy fighting off the hordes, enjoying life and being true to themselves.

I can also name lots of rock stars who fit into this category. Years of sex, drugs and rock and roll have taken their toll, but it doesn't stop the fans dropping at their feet. You might think, well, they're rock stars, so what do you expect? But would they have become rock stars and be as popular as they are if they didn't have the confidence to pull it off in the first place? I doubt it. If they had allowed their lack of good looks to keep them down, they wouldn't have had the balls to get on stage and make it happen.

Here's a fun exercise.

Imagine if a rock star took over your body. How differently would you act? What would you do differently? How would you speak? When you re-entered your body a few weeks later, how many more friends would you have? How much more respect would you have? How many more admirers would you have? How many more phone calls would you receive? (The picture texts might get interesting!)

It's not what you look like; it's how you act and feel that matter.

Through history, the faces that remain icons of beauty have been faces that broke the mould, not ones who conformed. Lady Gaga, just like Grace Jones and Barbara Streisand, will be remembered for her uniqueness. It's also people's ability to embrace that uniqueness that makes them distinctive and memorable.

You're as attractive or unattractive as you tell yourself you are! Nobody else can tell you whether or not you're attractive unless you give them that power. And you shouldn't. You should keep this power locked deep within your inner self.

As you feed this inner power by developing your 'can't care' mentality, watch how quickly your social confidence grows. You'll also see how differently people treat you, how much of an impact you have, and the amount of respect you get. Either way, you can't care about all this. These are just nice side-effects to what is really important: how you feel about yourself.

Open up to your insecurities

The definition of insecurity is 'uncertainty or anxiety about oneself'. Socially confident people know what their shortcomings and insecurities are and don't try to hide them. They put them out there for the world to see. People who try to hide their shortcomings are the most socially awkward and anxious.

As I previously mentioned, socially confident people are happy to laugh at themselves and not take themselves so seriously. Insecure people will do everything they can to stop the world from knowing what their insecurities are. If one of those insecurities is brought up, or a subject close to it is mentioned, they'll want the floor to swallow them up. It will become immediately apparent through their body language how much they're affected, which makes the insecurity ten times worse than it needs to be. (Think of the elephant in the room.)

Obvious examples of trying to cover up insecurities about physical aspects of yourself are comb-overs or wearing an ill-fitting wig, or having extreme cosmetic procedures like too many collagen injections to give you a trout pout, and teeth that glow in the dark. Intangible examples include being passive-aggressive, constantly putting people down, being overly funny in public and having the need to show everyone how great you are via extravagant material possessions.

When you open up to your insecurities, you will start loving yourself a bit more. Rather than feeling that instant dread when an insecurity is brought up, it won't bother you. You'll smile and joke about it (sincerely). There will always be an elephant in the room. The more you try to pretend it's not there, the more uncomfortable it will get. It will be like trying to cover the elephant with a tea cosy. Everyone knows it's there. People aren't stupid. More importantly, *you* know it's there. Mask it no more. Jump on the elephant and take it for a spin. You'll have so much more fun.

Your environment

Your journey of self-awareness will highlight the fact that
you are your environment. 'Your environment' means the
people you spend the most time with (friends, family and
colleagues) and the places you spend the most time (home,
work, school, etc.). All these things are major contributing
factors to who you are and how you feel on a daily basis.

Toxic people fall into our environment. They aren't one of
the obvious things we think of when it comes to dealing with
social anxiety (or any type of anxiety). But by being able to
spot them, and having the tools to protect yourself against
them, I hope you will be astonished and amazed by how
different your life will be. It's part of the defensive strategy
you need for the long-term changes you're looking for.

'It's business'

Do you ever get tired of hearing 'It's business' or 'It's not
personal, it's just business'? I know I do. In our culture, we've

somehow made it OK to crap on our fellow man/woman by saying it's nothing personal. But I've got news for you: it ain't just business. If someone does the dirty on you and masks it as being 'just business', they're still toxic.

There is nothing wrong with a bit of healthy competition. It's motivating. When someone new joins the company it's healthy to evaluate them and wonder how much of a threat they're going to be to you. That's survival. But if you intentionally go out of your way to sabotage them, that makes you toxic, even if you excuse it by saying you're doing it to get a foot on the career ladder. If you decide to act in a way that makes you immoral and unscrupulous, that means that you're an immoral, unscrupulous person. There are no ifs or buts.

Contrary to popular belief, you don't have to be immoral to succeed in your career, business or in life. In situations that call for tough decisions, it's good to be able to look subjectively at things, but you don't need to lose your conscience. Winning, beating the system, building your career, securing your financial future and growing a business does not have to involve being ruthless and immoral.

So you got a promotion by shafting your colleagues in the process. *Yay.* It got you a £5k pay rise (most of which you'll pay in tax). *Yay.* You get to boss a few more people around – the same people you shafted and who now despise you. *Yay.*

Was it worth it? We can't blame our primeval instinct to want to grow, survive and beat the competition to be the 'winner'. But greed – that's something else. Being immoral and unscrupulous is a choice.

If you've had the misfortune to be affected by a person led by greed, take comfort from the following:

- They act in this way with a very short-sighted point of view. Bending the rules might get them a short-term 'win', but it is not a win in the long run. They'll lose their friends, be paranoid, and may suffer health problems in the long term.
- It's likely they won't sleep as soundly at night as they would have you believe. A cocktail of prescription drugs is usually needed to clear their conscience and ease their anxiety to get a few hours of sleep.
- The reason they decide to go to war with their competitors rather than accept that competition can be healthy is down to their own deep insecurity and distinct unhappiness.

Let's not be naive. These people exist, and they exist in abundance. Should all us decent, kind folk pack our bags and go hiking in the Tibetan mountains to discover our inner spirit and avoid these unscrupulous people? Should we just leave these sociopaths to fight it out between themselves? Maybe. But we've got bills to pay too.

We might have to live with these folk, but we don't have to play their games. We can decide to handle our social anxieties better by rising above it all – by understanding that shafting your fellow man isn't a necessity to win. Even better, we can teach our kids that they can be decent human beings as well as succeed in their careers, in business, and in life. We can help them understand that if people choose to act in other ways, they are the real long-term losers.

For the ones who are thinking, 'That just means my kids will be the ones who get shafted by these people', I hear you. But this just feeds into the system I'm talking about. If you're aware enough to teach your kids about the importance of treating people well, living well, and being able to sleep at night, there's a strong chance they'll grow up savvy enough to know when the unscrupulous are shafting them. Plus, they'll be strong and wise enough to know how to do things their way. The alternative is a continuous cycle of people being taught that the more immoral you can be, the better. Social anxieties and insecurity will plague the younger generation like never before. Some people might call this hell on earth.

Revenge isn't sweet

Here's a classic quote by Albert Einstein:

'Weak people revenge.
Strong people forgive.
Intelligent people ignore.'

I've had the misfortune of dealing with people, both in
business and my personal life, who have built their lives on
getting revenge on their enemies. To these people, winning
isn't enough. They have to see everyone else lose for them to
feel they have won. Fundamentally, they are very unhappy
people. (If they were happy, they would be busy living their
own lives, rather than trying to destroy others.)

We all want to see someone who has done us wrong get a
piece of what they dished out. But let me ask you this: How
does getting revenge on someone make you feel? If your
initial reaction is 'good', you're thinking about the end result.
I'm talking about all the hours, days, weeks (and maybe even
years and decades) you spent pacing up and down in anger,
thinking 'How dare they think they can do that to me?' and
'I'll show them'. The end result might make you feel good
(for about a minute), but think of all the time you invested
and wasted in feeling like crap. Revenge just ain't worth it.
Revenge makes you care too much. Revenge isn't sweet.

However you look at it, revenge only brings about negativity
and the worst in people. Not just from you, but also from
everyone it involves. Revenge is built on nothing but pride,
which is why, like Einstein says, 'Weak people revenge'. It

takes a strong person to forgive, and it takes an incredibly intelligent person to ignore. Albert's quote is absolutely spot-on, so let's look at it in a little more detail.

Why is it that only weak people revenge?

Because revenge is built on pride. Pride is a sin for a reason. Putting aside the religious connotations, pride is a sin because of how it makes you feel. It is driven by your ego.

Revenge is stupid. An eye for an eye leaves us all blind! Revenge is like drinking poison and waiting for the other person to die. All revenge does, with the anger and resentment it causes, is eat away at us.

Is it worth being top dog if you're miserable, sad and lonely? What does 'winning' mean? Allowing anger and hate to consume you for hours, days, weeks, or even years? If your life is built on revenge, you're weak. Your energy is being drawn into a negative cycle. Your energy would be much better spent elsewhere.

Why is it only strong people can forgive?

Because forgiveness takes every ounce of strength you have. It goes against our instincts, which are driven by pride and ego. When we battle these instincts (which takes great strength), we realise it is much healthier for us not to be driven by these negative emotions. We're happier and freer when we let go of the anger and resentment – and we let go of it by forgiving.

If someone does something to you, it's in your ego's interest to react in retaliation. But doing this with the sole aim of 'getting back at someone' will make you no better than them. Moving on from someone or a situation you believe doesn't deserve your time or effort is not weakness. It's the opposite. Being focused and concentrating on what you're doing, with the sole purpose of moving on with your life, is strength. It might be perceived as weakness to the other person, but that's because they're trapped in a negative spiral. Leave them. Move on.

Forgiveness is freedom – for you, not them.

You don't forgive because you're weak. You forgive because you are the better, more intelligent person. You know that all the negativity that comes with revenge isn't worth it.

Why is it that only intelligent people can ignore?

Because deliberate ignorance is the cleverest tool of them all. Few of us use it because we're blinkered by anger and the need to revenge that is driven by our ego. The most hurtful thing someone can do is ignore you, act as if you're not in the same room. The most painful thing you can do to an ex-partner is move on with your life as if they were never in it.

Ignorance starves the bully of what they desire: attention. Why does a bully do what they do? Because they get the attention they crave. Crying and pleading with a bully doesn't work. These are forms of attention that arouse the bully and give them more reason to do what they do. When the bully is starved of attention, there is no fuel to stoke the fire. The fire burns out and they move on to their next victim. That victim will remain a victim until they decide not to stoke the fire with attention.

We have to face the facts: there are people on this planet, including bullies, who get joy from hurting others. Sometimes you can't reason with these people, making ignoring them the only intelligent solution. (If you want to know how to practically implement this strategy, I have that covered in the next chapter, 'A turd in the punchbowl'.)

Einstein's quote is great, but let's be brutally honest about forgiveness. Some people have done bad things and they don't deserve your forgiveness. Everything in you will tell you to revenge. Your ego will plague you and tell that if you don't do something in retaliation, you're weak and they've won. At times, you will find it hard to ignore your ego and the need to get revenge. But ultimately, you have a choice. You can focus your energy on yourself and the people you care about, or you can consume yourself with anger and hate and, in turn, live your life full of resentment and discontent.

Throughout this book I've emphasised the fact that none of us is perfect. We've all pissed someone off at some point, intentionally or unintentionally. If you want to live a decent life – a life that involves work, family and friends (basically, people) – pissing people off is unavoidable. The only way you can avoid it is if you live a life of solitude in the hills. Conflict is part of life – and it isn't a bad thing as long as the intention isn't to hurt others. Sometimes, conflict means you've stood up for something that you believe in. So there is most definitely a balance to be found. The key to getting the balance right is what I just said: Go about *your* business. Do what is right for you, without intentionally hurting someone else. If you do something that someone doesn't like (which will happen), how they react is up to them. That's none of your business. You can't care about that. If they choose to play games or seek revenge, that is also their choice. Just like it's your choice whether or not you play their games.

Weak people revenge.

Strong people forgive.

Intelligent people ignore.

Make the right choice.

It's not about you

When you stop to think about it, **nothing is ever personal**. We all act based on our own circumstances and our own needs. So, if someone treats you like crap, it's because *they* feel like crap. It might be because of something that happened to them in the past. Or you might have done something to annoy them. But if they're happy and content, they won't react.

Have you noticed that when things are going your way and life is good, the small things don't bother you? But when you're pissed off and angry, the smallest thing can set you off? The reason for this is simple. When we feel like crap, we want others to feel like crap too. We have plenty of excess crap to throw around. When we're happy and content, we can't care.

As an example, let's take personal appearance. There is nothing more hurtful than when someone insults the way you look. Your immediate reaction is a burst of anger. And rightly so. What gives anyone the right to make a comment on the way they look? But rein in your anger: **it's not about you – it's about them**. If someone comments on how you look, it's because they're insecure about the way *they* look. If someone makes an underhand or spiteful remark about anything, it's because they're insecure about something in their own lives.

Think of it like a big insecure mirror.

If someone ever makes a nasty comment to you, rather than act in anger, make yourself feel better instantly by knowing that a person's insults are a direct reflection on themselves. Imagine a giant mirror in front of them. They are putting the insult out because of their own reflection – what *they* see and how *they* feel inside. The more insults someone throws out, the more insecure they are. The worse the insult, the worse they feel and the harder they'll try to make themselves feel better.

Forget about getting angry. When you're dealing with someone challenging, your only concern should be about how you feel. If you react angrily, later you'll regret letting them get to you. You rewarded their bad behaviour with attention.

We all do things because of the way *we* feel. This is something to consider when choosing your environment, including the people you have in your life. When someone gives out kindness, it's because they have enough to dish out. That's the sort of person you want to associate with. We can all do with a bit more of that.

The biggest cock

There is always a reason why someone will treat you badly or insult you. The term 'pecking order' originated with chickens. It relates to the biggest cock showing his dominance by pecking all the other cocks underneath him into submission. Humans do the same thing, but we do it verbally as well as physically. When we insult someone, it's our way of 'pecking' them down. We're trying to establish ourselves as the biggest cock. (That has a double meaning.)

The reason someone puts you down could date back as far as their childhood. Or they might be jealous of what you've achieved. Who cares? You can't care. Just remind yourself that they're acting in that way for reasons that have nothing to do with you.

It's also worth noting that you can't give something you haven't got. If you don't feel happy, you can't make other people happy. Why would you want to see other people sipping cocktails on holiday or dancing at a party when all you want to do is punch a hole in the wall? You might smile superficially and ask to see the photos, but the hate is still in your eyes. That's why social media can induce such anxiety and depression. When you're at work, chained to your desk and surfing the net, seeing friends enjoying themselves on holiday can be depressing.

Feeling like this doesn't make you a bad person. It takes someone close to saint-like status to want to pass on good fortune when you have none. All you can do is go with the flow: accept the highs and the lows, while also appreciating you'll experience plenty of both. Both are temporary. Moods always are. If you're feeling down and socially anxious, it will pass. It always does.

Like attracts like

When you feel like crap, you want others to feel your pain. You want them to understand what you're going through. You feel better around other people who are angry and moaning, if you're in that kind of mood. And when you're on top of the world, you want to share that joy with other happy people. You don't want to be around unhappy people, who will quickly bring you down.

Have you noticed, when one of your friends is having a bad time, they avoid your usual meet-ups? Maybe you've done it yourself. When we feel down in the dumps, most of us would rather go through the pain in private, in the comfort of our home. If we have a partner or children, they can get the brunt of it. They don't have a choice – they live with you. Your friends are luckier. They don't live with you and can avoid the misery!

Remember what we said about your environment, and the fact that you are your environment? There is nothing wrong with going through varying emotions and ups and downs – it's natural. You just need to be mindful of when you might be getting sucked too far down. It's easy to feel bad and wallow. There's usually a queue of people waiting to join you in your misery, and you'll all feed off each other. The negative buffet is all you can eat, and there's plenty to go around.

Our need to be around like-minded people is why friendships and groups of friends change all the time, and why we tend to attract the same type of people as ourselves. When you're growing and becoming more self-aware and socially confident, you naturally find yourself attracting new people into your life who share your values. Positive attracts positive. Negative attracts negative.

If you find yourself with negative people, you'll be influenced to act negatively yourself. In that case, find yourself a different pack. Your environment sets your mood and the tone of your life. *You are your environment.* Think about who inspires you. What is it about them that inspires you? Are they action takers? Are they good at turning negatives into positives? Draw from that inspiration. If you want to be encouraged to moan, stay around people who make it a habit to moan.

Eventually, most of us appreciate the fact that there's more to life than moaning about trivial stuff. The first step to fixing this scenario is to find a new group of friends who share those values. If you choose to do that, you're listening to yourself and doing what you need to be a better, more confident, less socially anxious person. If that induces feelings of guilt to start with, it will soon pass when you appreciate life is offering you more.

A turd in the punchbowl

People who bring you down (or try to bring you down) are what I call 'toxic people'. I like the word 'toxic'. I think it sums up certain people and their behaviour very well. If you think about how toxicity works, it's very similar to how the wrong people in your life act towards you. The most obvious is the negative effect their behaviour has on you, and how easily and quickly the toxicity can spread.

A toxic person could be somebody very close to you – a parent, partner, boss, friend, sibling, colleague, teacher, anybody. The odds are, you have toxic people in your life right now. Everybody has. Toxic people affect us all; nobody is immune. Some are easy to recognise because their toxicity oozes out of them through their words and actions. Some are a little less obvious, which is why it's important to recognise their traits.

Being able to recognise and deal with toxic people will transform your life. As soon as you start to deal with the toxicity, it will feel as though a huge weight has been lifted off your shoulders. You'll no longer have to wear a mask and pretend to be somebody you're not. You'll feel like a brand-new person. Your social confidence will hit an all-time high.

As I've said before, nobody is perfect. We all have bad days, right? We all like a gossip and have a bit of toxicity in us. Confusing toxic behaviour with normal, everyday behaviour can lead to you cutting *everybody* out of your life, which is why I've defined what I mean by a toxic person here.

Toxic people:
- Always have drama in their life
- Rarely have anything good to say
- Are quick to criticise and judge others
- Are passive-aggressive
- Are very often jealous
- Are manipulative
- Lie a lot, and exaggerate the truth
- Have to win
- Rarely, if ever, apologise
- Don't see anything wrong in what they do
- Act as judge and jury
- Play the victim
- Care too much about what people think (but pretend they're not bothered)
- Make you feel like you need to prove yourself
- Intentionally look to destroy things that don't fit their purpose

- Hold grudges
- Show up when they're least expected
- Use privately shared information against you
- Are unpredictable
- Are narcissistic and delusional
- Have few friends
- Will bring you down to their level.

This is a pretty comprehensive list, but toxic people have lots of other characteristics and behaviours. Like a turd in a punchbowl, they have the awesome ability to mess up the nicest of things. A party. (Any social gathering, really.) A relationship. Your life. A bowl of punch. Nothing is immune to them.

It's the last point in the above list that is the most important, because toxic people will bring you down without remorse or hesitation. Toxic people can be so powerful that they can drag the nicest people into their clutches, sometimes without them seeing it coming. Then they'll keep you trapped in the negative cycle of social anxiety. They'll have you believe that you are nothing. That you are worthless.

Identifying toxic behaviour in your life, and doing something about it, will save you from unhappiness. Why? **Because toxic people are like sinking ships**. Their lives are a mess, and they have no problem with taking everybody else down with them. In fact, it's exactly what they want. *If I'm unhappy and miserable, then so should you be.*

Don't take it personally. It rarely has anything to do with a specific person. It's more to do with the fact that toxic people thrive on drama – so they make it their job to create drama – in all areas of life. That's why you'll find toxic behaviour in all walks of life: at work, at home, at school, everywhere – even when you go on holiday. Drama is always waiting around the corner, and if you're in the vicinity, you'll be swept along with it.

It makes sense: toxic people tend to associate with other toxic people, and this increases the chances of drama. If it isn't them directly causing the drama, somebody else in their life is, so it's still going to have an effect. If you're the one closest to them (because you are one of the few people who tolerates them and their behaviour), you'll bear the brunt of their dysfunctional behaviour. The longer you put up with it, the worse it gets, until you become their full-time lackey.

The way a toxic person hurts others isn't always obvious, unlike with verbal and physical abuse. It could manifest itself as not taking the time to play with or care for their child, for example, preferring instead to go to the pub. They might prioritise buying booze or fags over buying food for their family. They might place their needs before those of people who depend on them financially and emotionally. These are

147

some of the worst forms of toxic behaviour because if you're a kid, you're totally dependent on your parent/guardian to provide for you.

I could give many examples of toxic behaviour but, rather than get swept up in all that, let's focus on the solution. If you find yourself dealing with a toxic person, there's only one truly effective way of dealing with it.

Cut it out

There are lots of methods to use to deal with a toxic person and their unscrupulous ways. Counselling. Communicating. Confrontation. Moving. But the most effective way is to cut the toxicity out of your life.

Cutting out somebody close to you, like a family member or friend, is not easy. If that person is dependent on you and vulnerable, it makes it twice as hard. It's likely the toxic person has come to depend on you. You are one of the very few people who puts up with their behaviour and put-downs. If you decide that you're not going to put up with this behaviour any longer (good for you), and you manage that by cutting them out of your life, you've changed their world. You might have been her meal ticket. Maybe you were his punch bag. You could have been the person he took out all his insecurities and frustration on – like when he'd had a bad day at work and you got the brunt of it at home.

Cutting out a toxic person is hard, but once you break free, it's worth it. Your social anxiety will instantly decrease. You'll rekindle interests you lost previously. You'll reconnect with people you might have lost contact with. You'll rediscover passions and favourite pastimes – the ones you couldn't do because the toxic relationship got in the way.

As I mentioned, there is no easy way of cutting someone out of your life. All you can do is be open and honest, and tell them why you've come to this decision. It's then up to you to make sure you enforce your decision by cutting off all communication, both on- and offline. As time progresses, the lack of communication and interaction will get easier for all of you. You have to be strong. And you shouldn't feel bad. Did he feel bad when he was treating you the way he did? I very much doubt it. Eventually, he will find someone else to spread his toxicity to.

It's about doing what is right for you. The purpose of this book is to boost your social confidence so you can free yourself from social anxiety (caring too much about what people think). Never underestimate the effect that a toxic person can have on your progress. Dealing with toxic people in your life could be the thing that makes *all* the difference to you.

Can people change?

Experience has shown me that, if somebody *really* wants to change, they will. If they don't, they won't. There are lots of factors that contribute to this, and if you're in their life, you'll be one of them. If you're not enough of a reason for them to want to change, there is nothing you can do about it. If you've told them time and time again that you're fed up with their put-downs but they continue to ignore you, there is only so much communicating you can do before you have to take action.

Apart from judging somebody on their previous actions, here are some questions to ask yourself if you're considering cutting someone out of your life.

Can you forgive them for what they've said or done? If you can't, it's likely you'll end up demonstrating toxic behaviour yourself. If you can't leave the past where it is, there is no moving forward.

Are you sad when you're not with them? Cutting someone out will leave a hole in anybody's life, but is your life worse when they're not around? Do you put up with them because you're lonely? Loneliness isn't enough of a reason to keep someone in your life.

Does it hurt your pride to think you have to make the first move? Are you always the first to apologise? Pride has no place in a decent relationship, and feeling this way is a strong indication that the relationship isn't right.

Do they make you feel guilty? Guilt isn't the right reason to keep someone in your life. Toxic parents are especially good at this. 'I gave birth to you and you owe me everything' is a common, guilt-inducing statement used by a toxic parent. You don't owe anyone anything, especially someone who makes you feel guilty for not being in his or her life.

Are you less or more effective without them? Do they make you feel stressed, insecure, anxious, guilty or unloved? Or do you lack motivation and get-up-and-go when they're not around? If you do, maybe they were better for you than you thought.

Stick to your ultimatums

If you've been dealing with toxic behaviour for a while, it's likely that you haven't established boundaries. If you had, the problem might have already been solved. Not having boundaries gives toxic people a licence to treat you in any way they see fit. Setting boundaries tells everybody else exactly what you're willing to put up with. This is a crucial part of your 'can't care' mentality.

You can relax your boundaries with people you know you can trust. We all need to let our hair down every now and again, and being around the people you trust will help you do that (another reason why surrounding yourself with like-minded people is healthy for you). With anybody you deem toxic in any way, put your boundaries back up. You may have to deal with toxic people regularly, like at work, for example, and practising putting up your boundaries will help you.

Typical examples of putting your boundaries up include saying 'no' to a toxic boss who regularly asks you to work late; cutting a conversation short when a toxic friend is gossiping; and telling a toxic parent to back off when they're trying to control you and tell you how to live your life (and you're forty-six).

To help set boundaries, imagine a fort that runs all the way around you. Maybe this fort has a moat. This is your boundary, and if anybody crosses it, either physically or emotionally, you will act to defend it. (I'm not talking about violence here. Toxic behaviour doesn't solve toxic behaviour.) By setting your boundary (your fort and your moat), you're making it clear to anybody who wishes to treat you negatively that it won't be tolerated.

Unlike a real moat, toxic people won't fall into it, but you can guarantee they will try to breach it. It's up to you to decide what detoxifying methods will work best for that, including the option of cutting them out your life. It's also up to you to stay strong and not allow your fort to be taken over. If you decide that your boundary has been breached enough, and you decide to cut the behaviour out of your life, remember the toxic person has chosen to be toxic. It's natural for you to feel guilty, or feel that you are abandoning them. You're not. You're becoming the best person you can be, and if that means cutting toxic people out of your life, so be it. You've outgrown their behaviour, and it's time to move on with your life. You'll quickly get over this feeling because (1) you have nothing to feel guilty about, and (2) you'll feel much better afterwards.

If you don't stick to your ultimatums, you'll be seen as weak – weaker than before – and you might find that the behaviour gets worse. The put-downs and treatment will get more severe. If you fail to stick to an ultimatum, you're telling your partner/friend/boss/kid that they can do what they like – and they'll continue to get away with it. If your kid keeps climbing up to reach the biscuit tin, and you keep telling them to stop without enforcing any ultimatum, they will keep on climbing.

Your common sense should tell you if the person deserves a chance, or more than one chance. This will depend on the person, their actions, how well you know them, and how much you love them. You then have to be strong – to make sure you go through with what you have decided to do.

Consider other people's thoughts, feelings and needs – but not to the detriment of your own health and well-being.

People can get frustrated when they believe that they can somehow control the toxic people in their life. If you haven't discovered by now, this isn't how it works with a toxic person. The more you try to influence them using reason, the more disillusioned you'll become. Reduce your stress and anxiety by remembering **you can only control yourself and your actions; you can't control anyone else.**

Toxic people will do their best to control you and dictate how you do things, where you go, who you see and what you do. It's up to you to put them straight. The more you do it, the more they'll get the picture, until they realise that trying to control you is futile. *You* are in absolute control. If you don't want to do something, don't do it. If you don't like the options on the table, suggest your own option, or walk away.

If you're worried about the consequences of your disobedience, get more control by planning your moves and stay one step ahead. There is more of a consequence if you put up with whatever it is you don't want to do. The more you do that, the more your independence will slip away, until it's completely gone. You'll stay trapped in that cycle of social anxiety.

Not taking control – allowing things to go on as they are – will mean either nothing will change, or things will continue to get worse. You have to be willing to take charge of your life, your well-being and your mental health. Nobody else is responsible for these things.

Authentic confidence

The reason you're reading this book is to find out how to free yourself from social anxiety. That means learning to stop worrying so much about what people think – and learning to care less in general. There is something intrinsic to making this happen, and it's all linked to what I call *authentic confidence*.

Remember that veneer-type confidence I mentioned earlier – the type that only lasts for a few days or hours? The confidence you gain from getting a compliment, a small pay rise, or the phone number of someone you fancy? This is all veneer-type stuff. You can't build a future on it. If you depend on this type of superficial confidence to keep you going, you're heading for a fall.

Think of it like building a house. You wouldn't build a house on a weak foundation. Yet, most of us are building our lives on one. It doesn't take much for the house to come crumbling down. An insult will do the trick. Someone says something mean to you, and it's enough to make you want to hide in your bedroom with the blankets over your head.

Your weak foundation (lack of substance) will make you react emotionally to the smallest of things – things that you should be able to shrug off. The house (your life) needs a stronger foundation, so you can withstand the hardship and challenges that come with life and the people in it. The way to get that stronger foundation is through authentic confidence.

The definition of confidence is 'the feeling or belief that one can have faith in or rely on someone or something'. Let's break this down. It means that confidence is a feeling or belief. What does this mean to you? It tells me that confidence is a choice. For example, I could be in a situation where I should not feel confident at all, yet, if I believe I'm confident and feel it, I am. *In-ter-est-ing, Mr Bond.* (Said with a villain accent while stroking my cat.) This means I could be walking around the supermarket sporting a cow-patterned onesie, all eyes on me, and if I felt confident, there would be no problem. I wouldn't be embarrassed. This reinforces my earlier point about what embarrassment truly is: *our own perception.*

When I use the logical gap to keep my ego at bay, I have a choice about how I feel. That means, if confidence is a feeling, I can *choose* to be confident. So the first significant message is this: **You have absolute power and choice over how confident you are** – whatever situation you're in.

The second significant message I get from this definition is: **If you can rely on yourself, nothing and no one can make you feel insecure.** In other words, if you can develop your authentic confidence to the point that you believe in yourself wholeheartedly, and know that your opinion counts the most, you can handle anything that comes your way – including other people, what they say and what they think.

I discovered these truths about five years ago. I've been putting them into practice ever since, and I can tell you that they work. Over time, they've allowed me to transform from being anxious, indecisive and insecure to having a 'can't care' mentality that involves self-control and authentic confidence. I used to walk around as that weak house I mentioned. I was ready to topple at any second: I was vulnerable and open to the elements. Now my shutters are closed, my moat is built, and my house is built on steel foundations. It would take a pretty hefty wolf to blow it down.

I never believed that I'd be confident enough to perform our consistent #1 fear (public speaking), but now I'm happy to get on stage and do my thing in front of thousands of people. I've spoken at venues as large as football stadiums – because I understand that (a) I have absolute power and choice over how confident I am, and (b) I can rely on myself, so no one else can make me feel insecure.

To make the most of these truths about confidence requires nothing more than a shift in mindset that we are *all* capable of making. If your natural inclination is to get embarrassed in public, you just have to unravel that habit using those two truths I've just shared. If these truths aren't enough, I show you below how to implement them. But rest assured that this knowledge, if you let it, will be life-changing.

Your shift in mindset (your new 'can't care' mentality) won't happen overnight. It's like learning a new language. First of all, you have to become aware of the language you already speak, and the new language you want to learn. (In this instance, the language you already speak includes ego, fakery and pretence. The language to learn is authentic confidence, including the ability to be yourself.) Then you have to put it all into practice. With time and practice, you will become fluent. Like learning a new language, some of you will take to it better than others. Some will learn fast, some will need more time, and some will say, 'Screw this, this is way too much hassle!' Be careful, though: saying this will take you straight back to what you've always done and how you've always felt. Be patient and give yourself time.

Why do you keep saying 'authentic' confidence?

Throughout my research for this book, and along my journey of discovery, I've paid particular attention to confidence and how it works. This has meant me scrutinising how I think and act – and how others think and act. From this, I've come to realise there are two types of people. (From a psychological point of view, there are lots more, but I like to keep things simple.) These are (1) the authentically confident, and (2) fakers. There is a fine line between the two, but the difference in their quality of life, including how fulfilled and happy they are, is vast.

Authentically confident people, or socially confident people, live with a sense of assurance and purpose that provides them with all the security and contentment they need. You know the type. They're happy and comfortable speaking to people, and when they're not, they will just as happily sit in the corner sipping a cup of coffee on their own, 'can't caring' less. They'll even do it without needing to show how busy and popular they are by playing on their mobile phone. (I know, crazy, right?)

Fakers, although they sometimes appear confident, live in a world full of anxiety, insecurity and doubt. Deep down, they are some of the unhappiest people you'll ever meet. Unfortunately, most of us, most of the time, fall into this 'faker' category. We put on a brave face when, deep down, we don't feel good.

For example, a faker tends to have lots of Facebook friends. They're very proud of this. The problem is, they haven't met most of these people in real life. When it comes to having real relationships with substance and trust, they fall short. 'Substance' is the key word here. Fakers lack substance in most areas of their lives.

Our mission is to give you authentic confidence. It's the type of confidence that gives you the substance you need to live a fulfilling life. To help form a better understanding of what authentic confidence is, so we know what we're aiming for, let's take a look at a few traits of authentic confident people and fakers.

Authentically confident people:

- Have a steely internal framework. (Think how Superman's internal organs might look.)
- Are the first to greet people, introduce themselves, and put out their hand in a public gathering.
- Get involved in a conversation, and sit inside the social circle.
- Have the ability to handle any situation they're in because they believe they can handle anything that comes their way.
- Appreciate and accept compliments.
- Don't need reassurance from others.
- Will happily stay silent in front of fools.

- Don't feel the need to shout from the rooftops about how fantastic their lives are. They're too busy living.
- Are not afraid to confront people if they know they have a valid point of view.
- See no point in judging others or putting them down.
- Enjoy taking risks but know when they've hit their limit. They're not afraid to say 'enough is enough'.
- Aren't afraid to admit to their mistakes.
- Know when they are being led by ego and pride.

Fakers:
- Operate from a weak foundation that is ready to collapse at any second. (Think fragile mind.)
- Avoid new introductions wherever possible.
- Cover up their insecurities by being extra-loud or trying too hard to be funny in a social environment.
- Are people-pleasers, which can lead to them being taken advantage of. Trying harder leads to frustration, anger and rage – emotions that are normally suppressed or directed towards loved ones.
- Avoid extra responsibility and prefer to dodge problems rather than deal with them head-on.
- Are easily overwhelmed by stress and anxiety.
- Feel uncomfortable when given a compliment, and will deflect it back at the giver in an insecure way.
- Avoid confrontation, and if they do confront someone, it's usually passive-aggressively rather than assertively. (A faker will confuse the difference

between being aggressive and assertive. For example, you'll find them picking on a waiter in a restaurant because they believe it makes them look powerful.)

- Seek comfort by judging others regularly and gossiping about people behind their backs.
- Hit the risk threshold but continue to add more risk to show others how they can handle it all. The pressure mounts to unworkable levels, and cracks soon appear through uncontrollable stress and anxiety.
- Hide away from their mistakes and try to cover them up by blaming others.
- Are easily led by their ego and pride, and let these things dictate who they are.

Ill health is another sure sign of internal issues suffered by fakers. Once, I was so ill I thought I was close to death. I had five episodes of tonsillitis within twelve months. (Well, that was what I was diagnosed with. On reflection, I'm not convinced.) It wasn't the usual kind of tonsillitis. I was bedbound, couldn't move, and my skin turned a strange shade of grey. I was prescribed six different types of antibiotic, none of which worked. I'm mentioning this here because at the time, I was very much a faker – a master faker, if you like. I was deeply unhappy and not dealing with my issues, including the toxic people in my life. My health only improved when I sorted my head out. A crucial part of this transition was increasing my authentic confidence.

I strongly believe that your health and well-being are entwined with how you think. If you'd told me that my thoughts were keeping me bedbound back then, I'd probably have called you a hippy and asked you to get me more medicine. So, when I tell people that their ill health is connected to how they're thinking, I understand why they don't always get it.

Denial is a powerful tool when you don't want to face the truth.

Denying the connection between how we think and feel could lead to frequent ill health. Your immune system won't be as effective as it can be. This is based on medical fact. When you're feeling low, your immune system is down. When you're being a faker, not saying what's really on your mind and pretending to be OK when you're not, you're not going to feel as strong as you could. That will decrease your immune system, and increase your chances of getting ill.

I used to be ill all the time. Since I've sorted my head out, I can't remember the last time I went to the doctor.

I never used to say what was on my mind. Maybe that's why my health issues were related to my throat. Or maybe it was just a coincidence. But what I am sure of is this: The older I get, the less I believe in coincidence.

No one is immune to what life throws at us. Everyone has good and bad days. We deal with different circumstances, so we naturally switch between authenticity and fakery for survival. Some days we'll feel like we can take on the world, and some days we won't want to get out of bed. That makes you human.

We all have environments where we feel at ease and confident, and other places where we feel uncomfortable. We can't expect consistency when it comes to how we feel and act. But in a general sense, you are either authentic or faking. The aim is to make your core more genuine than fake. When you do that, life gives you better health, better prospects, better people, better relationships and a better foundation to work from – in a nutshell, a much better existence.

Faking it – the right way

When I was trying to bridge the gap between being a highly anxious wreck and someone who can comfortably speak in public, I used a 'fake it till you make it' mentality. The *principle* behind faking it till you make it is very simple, but actually doing it is harder, which is why we're not all living a perfect life.

Think of it this way. What makes a great actor? What separates Leonardo DiCaprio from a part-time amateur dramatics performer? Lots of things, including talent, intelligence, opportunity and believability, right? But it's the last point (believability) that is the real power behind faking it till you make it. That's what we're going to focus on.

When you get more believable at what you do, reality catches up with the fakery. It's another way of saying **what you focus on, you get more of**. When you live a life based on pretence and ego, that's the life you get in return. When you choose to focus more on a life of fulfilment and substance, you get more of that. Faking it till you make it bridges the gap between what you want, and making it happen.

Let's say you're naturally quiet. When you attend meetings, you have great ideas, but you like to stay separate from the action. People have come to appreciate that you are quiet and it's highly unlikely you'll voice your opinion. But you're fed up with not being heard, and you want to start putting your ideas out there. Using the 'fake it till you make it' strategy, you decide to make a suggestion in the next meeting you attend. You practise what you're going to say in your head (just like any other good actor would), and you go ahead and deliver your idea as planned. It feels uncomfortable, but you decide to do the same thing in the next meeting. It stills feels unnatural, but you keep doing it in every meeting over the next three months. After three months of consistently voicing your ideas, your 'fakery' is now reality. People have come to appreciate you as a person who speaks up. More importantly, that uncomfortable feeling of shyness and social anxiety is also now a thing of the past. If you followed this process, not only for meetings but also for everything you wanted to change in your life, imagine how different you would feel and what you could achieve.

There's no magic in this. It comes down to *practice*. Have you ever asked someone, 'Are you nervous?' and they answered, 'No, I've done this a million times before'? Think about something you've done more than once, and how much easier it was to do the second or third time. Having kids, for example. I've got friends who say their first child was the hardest. That was the one they fussed over and wrapped in cotton wool. By the time the third or fourth kids were born, they were practically bringing themselves up!

Practice is what creates familiarity, and familiarity gets rid of nerves. That's why practice is key. If you stop doing something, you get rusty at it. The same applies for practising confidence. When you stop acting confident, you lose the skill.

Don't be fooled. Confidence is a skill, just like any other.

Do you think top sales people get to the top without practising the skill of influence? Do you think their ability to charm and persuade is something they just possess? It's not. They practise it. They see what language (verbal and body) works, and they continue to develop that, making their ability to influence stronger.

It's easy to view influence as a skill, yet we tend to view confidence as something else – almost like we're either born with it or we're not. That is BS. People are all born with different advantages; there is no doubting that. But confidence is a skill and, like all skills, it can be improved and developed – no matter how old you are. The good news is, it can be done fairly quickly. In fact, you can get instantly better at it simply by making the decision to get better at it. You do that by realising that confidence is a skill, not something you have zero control over. When you do that, things will change pretty quickly for you. I know they did for me.

I've broken this process down into three easy steps. It might help to write things down as you follow these steps.

STEP 1

Look at who you are right now, and who you want to be. What are the differences between the two? For example, are you quiet, and do you want to speak up more? Try to be as specific as possible about the changes you want. Relate your need to a specific event, like wanting to be more vocal in a business meeting. That will give you a goal to aim for.

STEP 2

Using a 'fake it till you make it' mentality, practise what you're going to say in the next meeting. (I'm following the example of being vocal in a meeting for continuation. Your example could be based on anything you like.) To help, you could copy or 'mirror' someone who is good at what you want to do. For example, do you have an assertive colleague? What do they say? How do they say it? Picture yourself communicating in a similar assertive way – one that suits you.

STEP 3

Consistently act the way you want to be. Get past the uncomfortable feelings. Don't give up. Reality will catch up with the 'faking', and the core of who you are will change.

In Hollywood, they call this method acting. Method acting is not only acting the part but also *being* the part – allowing yourself to be live the part, physically, mentally and emotionally. This helps actors to act in a way that gives the audience a sense of complete believability. The actor becomes the part – and it's small differences in their words, the way they're said, and how actors use their body to communicate that separate good actors from the all-time greats.

If it's not the small differences that count, then what does? All it takes is millimetres of difference to define somebody's face and the way they look. (There are nearly eight billion people on the planet, and we all look different. What does this take?) Just take a look at Formula One. These guys don't qualify and win in seconds. They win in milliseconds. The difference between pole position and tenth position is minuscule. It's the same in golf. If you hit the ball with a millimetre of misdirection, that ball is landing in the water. That's why the top golfer in the world is only ever so slightly better than the person ranked 100th. The same thing applies to most things in life. Generally, what separates the world's best from the average isn't that much. Isn't it good to know that you are minuscule steps away from transforming the way you feel?

The principles are the same as in faking it till you make it and method acting, but most of the 'acting' takes place in the mind. This is also called visualisation. A sprinter will imagine running past his opponents and crossing the line as the winner before the race starts. You might have seen a sprinter talking to himself and looking down to the finish line before the race starts? This is part of the visualisation process. He's celebrating his victory in his mind before the race has started.

You can't win a race unless you *believe* you can win. Everything starts with belief.

Whatever you want to call it, I want belief in yourself to form part of your new 'can't care' mentality.

The simple three-step process I shared is all anybody does to achieve what they want. An actor, athlete, architect or author all follow the same process. You can try to overcomplicate it as much as you like, but this is what fulfilment looks like. If you want to grow your authentic confidence, ditch your social anxiety and become the person you want to be, it's the path you have to take.

That three-step process is about faking it the right way – but you can also fake it in the wrong way. That's like building a house (your future) on marshland. That's dangerous and pointless. So, when you're faking it till you make it, you've got to keep a keen eye on substance. Let's take a quick look at substance and how to make sure we keep it.

Substance

In a world of pretence and unhappy fakers, there is no doubting the importance of keeping the core of who you are intact. We do that by keeping our core full of substance – packing it out with hard-core to make it solid. The 'hard-core' in this instance is all the authentic confidence qualities we covered. I keep making house-building analogies, but they seem to fit here.

If you build a house on marshland, it will topple. If you build a house on a strong foundation, it will last. So: build your future on pretence and you will topple. Build your future with substance, and it will last.

Faking it till you make it could be seen as having no substance, because if you're faking, you're still not being true to yourself. A valid point. But here's the deal. Faking it till you make it – in the *right* way – is different because you're aware that you want change. You're acting like the person you want to become, so the acting is intentional. Problems arise when we're acting to impress others – like when we buy things to impress other people. This creates the pretence and shallow personality we're talking about.

When you do something for the sake of impressing others, there is a lack of substance. When you do it for

yourself with intent and purpose, it's *real* and full of substance.

This means that we have to do more of the things we want to do for the right reasons to get more substance. The more we do things to impress other people, the more we'll be trapped in the cycle of social anxiety. Asking yourself why you're doing something before you do it will stop this from happening.

Is imitation the same as faking?

In step two of my three-step process, I mentioned mirroring. You've probably heard the idea that, if you imitate (or 'mirror') one of the greats, you'll become great yourself. I have mixed views about this, but there could be some truth in it.

If your idol is Michael Jackson, for example, learning how to dance like him doesn't necessarily mean you're going to become the next worldwide pop sensation. What worked for Michael might not work for you. And that's where this notion falls short.

There is a lot of common sense in copying the greats rather than imitating somebody who has never achieved anything. You might admire your dad, but if he's unhappy and unfulfilled in his sixties, is it wise to copy him? There's always a better way to do something, and if someone has discovered it and done it well, why spend your time trying to reinvent the wheel?

If you want substance and authentic social confidence, some originality will go a long way. Imitating alone won't work. Extraordinary people are extraordinary because they are unique. You are unique. Embrace your unique qualities to enhance your substance. Start by thinking about what you're good at and what you enjoy doing. These things are clues to expanding on your uniqueness and potential greatness.

When you're faking it till you make it, by all means, look at what your idols have done, how your CEO chairs a meeting, and how your mum makes the perfect cake. Take the best bits of advice and guidance, and use them, but don't forget to be yourself – your wonderful, unique self.

Leverage

This penultimate chapter is a bonus chapter. So far, I've not discussed persuasion, but this chapter does – and for good reason! *Persuasion* and *influence* create better relationships, and help us to turn enemies into allies. The ability to influence people also plays a key role in helping you to overcome social anxiety and insecurity. It aids the type of authentic social confidence that builds the strong foundation you need for long-term change. It's also a handy skill that helps you get more of the things you want out of life, which is never a bad thing.

When you think about persuasion or influence, you might think of being influenced to buy something, such as a car. But it goes much deeper than that. Influence plays a part in everything we do, from the moment we get up in the morning to going to sleep at night. Landing the job you want, getting the love you crave from your partner, and persuading your screaming child to go to bed, all require influence. The better you are at it, the easier your life will be.

Some people believe that studying influence is a form of manipulation. They're right. There is a reason why influence isn't taught at school. You might take classes in science, maths, English and history, but there's no classroom for influence. Why? The government would have a pretty tricky time trying to manage a society of free-thinking master influencers. The ability to perform test tube experiments you'll never do after you leave school isn't doing too much harm. That skill is highly unlikely to start a revolution.

Influence is a form of self-education. In this chapter I intend to show you how to influence people – to help you reduce your social anxiety, boost your authentic social confidence, and help you get an edge over others when you need it. If you choose to use your newfound influencing skills to fulfil your ambition of being the next Frank Abagnale (the con man played by Leonardo DiCaprio in the film *Catch Me if You Can*), that's up to you. But I'm not too worried about that. The things we're about to cover won't quite get you to world-class con man level. They will, however, get you thinking about improving your influencing skills, including your body language and the words you choose. They might even get you a better deal on your next car purchase.

This doesn't mean the skill of influence should be abused. You're always going to get unscrupulous people taking advantage. But this shouldn't put you off. That's like saying you shouldn't learn maths because it would make you better at adding up than someone else. But where do you draw the line? It's up to you. There's a big difference between learning the skill of influence to get an edge in life (like winning a job interview) and using your knowledge to commit a crime or take advantage of somebody.

In my usual straightforward fashion, we'll sum up what persuasion is in one word. Persuasion is *leverage*. Forget everything you've learned about influence, what it means and how to get it. Influence simply comes down to how much leverage you have.

Leverage disguises itself in many forms. Money. Good looks. Advanced communication skills. Body language. Making love with gusto. All of this will get you leverage. (With the latter, I get a healthy top-up in the relationship leverage bank about once every two months. To expect more would be unrealistic. Give a guy a break.)

You'll hear the term 'leverage' used a lot in business, usually when negotiating. Whoever has the most leverage at the negotiation table will usually walk away with the best deal. Leverage is the reason some people get shafted, and others walk away more than satisfied. What we don't realise is how much leverage plays a part in everyday life. When we become aware of this, we can use it to our advantage.

Think of a relationship you have right now. It could be with your partner, a friend or family member. When you analyse the relationship, who would you say gets the most out of it? By this I mean meaningful things, like love and compassion. Things like money and material possessions are less meaningful because they have little substance. The term 'sugar daddy' relates to this type of relationship. Generally, the person giving more in the relationship has the least leverage, and the person receiving more has more leverage. Why? Because the person giving wouldn't give so much if they didn't feel they had to. Sound a little cold? You bet it is! People give out of love and kindness, but fundamentally, they give because they *have to* – this is born from a need to satisfy others and themselves.

Doing what we have to do in relationships is based on our survival instinct. If we feel we would struggle to survive without the relationship, we'll work harder to keep it. We might get complacent over time, but a sharp reminder of the prospect of a lonely life soon puts us back into line. 'I'm leaving you and taking the kids' is a loud wake-up call.

If the balance of leverage in a relationship you have is pretty even, you have a solid relationship. If you feel the relationship is one-sided, however, it's time to pay attention. The same applies in all areas of your life. Is your job worth the stress it causes? If it isn't, it won't be long before you're looking for a new job. The company you work for has lost its leverage with you.

Issues arise when you're the one giving and giving and getting very little in return. In this instance, you have little to no leverage. If this rings true for you, fear not. This can be fixed, and the good news is there are just two things why this might be happening.

1. You're allowing yourself to be treated like a fool.
2. You're being abused.

If you're allowing yourself to be treated like a fool, this will carry on until you address the issue. You need to make a conscious decision to stop being a fool by getting some of your leverage back. In a relationship, playing the fool might be forgiving a partner the fifth time he cheats. Or letting your partner spend every weekend away with his/her mates, leaving you at home with the kids.

We tend to play the fool for a few reasons, with the overriding one being that it suits us (at the time). We might find it easier because it means we don't have to take responsibility. Our partner might be the one who does everything and makes all the decisions, which makes for an easier life for us. We might also play the fool because we think that's what our partner wants. This is a form of extreme people-pleasing. Acting the fool needs to be addressed, as it will lead to a big fall. There is nothing worse than being left out in the cold with no leverage when the person with all the leverage decides they don't want you any longer.

There are exceptions to this rule of being a fool and being abused. If you're a kid being abused by a parent, you don't have much choice. You can't leave home. A child's lack of physical and mental leverage to change the situation is clear. Your environment, opportunities, and the people in your life will all dictate your standing. But every adult has the opportunity to leave to find something better. And you do this by getting more leverage.

Leverage is about putting yourself back in the driving seat by taking back control in your life. Having no leverage means you'll always be the passenger. Someone else will be in charge of where you're heading. Sometimes that's OK, but what happens when there is no one to drive the car? You only have yourself to blame if you haven't learned to drive yourself. That's dangerous, and will lead to social anxiety because you'll always depend on other people. Social confidence comes with independence.

Sitting back and thinking 'My husband/wife handles all that' could mean you're heading for a fall. It's OK to rely on people to do certain things. You can't do everything yourself. But if you're doing next to nothing for yourself, it's time to get some independence back. It's time to get a better balance of leverage.

Leverage (or persuasion) isn't about bending over backwards to get people on your side – that defeats the object. Eagles hunt alone, and they are the best in the business. Pigeons flock together because they have to. Alone, they are weak. They are easy prey. An eagle would peck a pigeon's head off. There's a saying: 'You'll always find a weak man in a crowd, and a wise man found alone.' I've always aspired to be more of an eagle than a pigeon. Weak people join groups. We turn to religion, cults and gangs when we're at our weakest, when we want (and need) to feel part of something. They prey on the most socially anxious people. It's nice to have strength in numbers and not to feel so alone, but you'll find plenty of other issues in groups like these. Rituals, bullying tactics and rigid 'my way or the highway' rules are enough for me to keep my distance from groups who act in this way.

If you depend on others to make you feel good, you're heading for a fall. Having leverage is about knowing that you could stand on your own two feet, if you had to. We're going to look at a few methods to help you increase your independence and leverage.

Here are four highly effective persuasion and influencing tools you can start using straightaway to get more leverage.

These tools amalgamate the skills that make the difference, rather than focus on all the clichés you'll find in other books. These tools will naturally increase your self-awareness (the ingredient needed to boost your authentic social confidence). You'll be a better communicator and a more powerful influencer and, most importantly, your leverage will grow.

Influence tool #1:
Think 'you', not 'I'

This is probably the best influence tool, so pay attention.

Do you remember the chapter 'Nobody cares'? They don't. People are only interested in what *they* want. You can choose to ignore or deny this, or you can embrace it and use it to your advantage.

Our survival instinct is continually checking what we want and need. What we want and need takes priority over what others want and need. We are naturally selfish creatures, thanks to our survival instinct. What's important to others, such as what our partners want, plays a part in our lives, but we tend not to do things if we don't feel we have to. We might go out of our way to buy flowers and chocolates at the start of a relationship, but we're less likely to do it six months into it. (Unless it's for a special occasion.)

Prioritising what others want and need over our own wants and needs keeps *them* alive, not you – and this goes against our nature. The only exception to this rule is when caring for a child. Adults are a different matter. Everything we do is based on gaining an advantage and avoiding pain. Your partner buys you flowers because he loves you, but also to avoid the pain of you thinking he's selfish for not thinking of you. *All my other friends got flowers, so why didn't I?* That could lead to many lonely nights spent in the spare bedroom. That would be painful, and your partner would prefer to dodge that pain, so they buy the flowers.

If you're still struggling with the notion that we're all selfish at our core, here are some more examples.

When you ask somebody what they do for a living, what you're really asking is, 'Will what you do for a living benefit me in some way? How much do you earn? Is it more than me? Are you higher on the social ladder than me? If you are, I need to give you more respect. If you're not, I can feel dominant and confident in your presence.' If you're looking for a partner at the time of asking, the answer will form part of criteria.

When you tell your child to be careful crossing the road, or tell your partner to take care when they go to work, what you're really saying is 'Don't get hurt because I couldn't handle it if you did.' The thought of them getting hurt is abhorrent to you, but a lot of that is because it would cause *you* emotional pain.

When you buy your partner flowers, what you're really saying is 'Let's move past the argument we had last night because I can't handle the stress of another one. I was an idiot and I acted like a twit. Sorry.' And then you won't have to sleep in the spare bedroom. The flowers represent a tangible way of moving past the pain. At the time of writing this, the UK flower industry is worth around £2.2 billion per year! To put that into perspective, the music industry is worth about £2 billion. That's a lot of pain avoidance!

Tell me this selfish stuff ain't true.

You can either resent the fact that everything relates to what we want (this includes you) or you can use it to your advantage. My advice is to do the latter, because this has the power to influence the steeliest of hearts and most stubborn of heads.

To show you how it works, I'm going to use an example of negotiation. We'll use a common one – buying a car. We'll start with a common negotiation, and compare it to a successful negotiation.

Common negotiation

Car salesman: 'So what do you think of the car?'

You: 'I like it.'

Car salesman: 'So if we can get the figures right for you, are you in a position to buy it today?'

You: 'Yes, but it'll depend on the price.'

You've both just left the car following your test drive, and you're sitting at his desk.

Car salesman: 'The car costs £25,000. For a deal today, we can take £500 off, making the monthly payment £550. Can we do a deal?'

You: 'Oh no, that's too expensive for me. I only have a budget of £400 a month. I need you to take more money off the car because I can't afford that.'

Car salesman: 'I can't do that, I'm afraid.'

The car salesman tries to offer you a cheaper car but you have your heart set on the car you drove. The negotiation falls apart and you walk away.

Successful negotiation

Car salesman: 'The car costs £25,000. For a deal today, we can take £500 off, making the monthly payment £550. Can we do a deal?'

You: 'I'm keen for us to make this deal work, but my budget doesn't stretch that far. What else can you do to make the deal work?'

Car salesman: 'There isn't a lot more I can take off for this car. My boss is keen to get some more sales before the end of the month, but I'm not sure we can do much more.'

You: 'Thanks for your honesty. Seeing as you're being so open and honest, how close are you to achieving your monthly sales target?'

Car salesman: 'Er, I think I need another two sales to achieve my target and hit my full bonus before Monday.'

You: 'My budget is £400 a month, and I'm in a position to put down the deposit and buy this car today. Let's do the deal to get you one car away from getting you your bonus. OK?'

Car salesman: 'Let me go and speak to my boss and see what I can do.'

I'm not into fairy tales, but there is no reason why the salesman wouldn't convince his boss to agree to this, or at least, agree to something very close to it – even though it's not the deal that *they* want. Why? Because you sold him the concept that the deal will work for *him* and his boss, rather than it working for *you*.

The first unsuccessful negotiation was focused on what *you* wanted and needed – so there were lots of 'I's'. If you remember what I said earlier, nobody gives two shits what you want, especially the car salesman. He is only interested in what he wants, and he wants the sale and his bonus. That's why, when you look at the successful negotiation, you'll notice a lot more 'you'.

By basing your negotiation around what *he* wants (the sale and bonus), rather than what *you* want (which he doesn't care about), you win.

If he came back after speaking to his boss and said there was nothing he could do, you'll know he's telling the truth. That would give you the option to take the deal at what you know is the best price, or decide to try your technique somewhere else. Do it enough, and you'll find the right deal.

Thinking 'you', not 'I', is a powerful technique in all aspects of your life, not just when buying a car. Think about how you might use it at home. Let's say your child won't eat her dinner. This used to be a regular occurrence in my house, and this is how I handled it.

It was a Saturday afternoon, and I'd made my daughter dinner, only for her to turn her nose up at the horrible-looking 'green things' on her plate. I tried gently educating her about the fact that the 'green things' would make her big and strong. I tried telling her how tasty they were if she would only give them a try. Out of sheer frustration, I also tried raising my voice to convince her. (This was before I discovered and implemented my logical gap technique.) None of it worked. She started crying, and wanted to leave the table, still hungry. Getting into a huff was a perfect reason for her not to have to eat the 'green things'. To her, it meant she could skip dinner and go straight to dessert. This same thing happened pretty much every dinnertime for the next week, until I decided to change tactic.

It was a Sunday. Earlier that day, we'd been to a summer fete. They had ponies at the fete, and my daughter was quick to point them out. It was the first time she'd had a pony ride, and she loved it. When it came to dinnertime that day, the usual behaviour started. 'I don't like the look of that. What are these weird-looking things?' This time, rather than start ranting about how ungrateful she was, I calmly asked her, 'Did you enjoy your pony ride earlier today?' Her face immediately changed. She smiled. 'Yes, I loved it.'
'Well,' I said, 'did you know that big girls who ride ponies eat their dinner every day? Otherwise, they wouldn't have the energy or strength to ride them.' She continued looking at me, and I could see I'd got her thinking. 'Would you like to ride a pony again?' I asked.
'Yes please!' she responded enthusiastically.
'Well, you'll have to eat all your dinner up, like the big girls who ride ponies do.' I walked away from the table, unsure if

my sly persuasion tactic would work. I could see her thinking for about another ten seconds. All of a sudden, she picked up her fork, and I'd never seen her eat so quickly. She ate everything on her plate – including the green things.

If you want to persuade somebody to do something, you'll only achieve it if they want to do it. People might not want to do what you want them to do, so it's up to you to persuade them using a language *they understand*. If someone doesn't understand you and the instructions you're giving, you're communicating in a way that works for *you*, not them. If you choose to take responsibility for that, and communicate in a different way – a way they understand – you'll get a better result.

The knack to getting this right comes down to you helping the person realise the benefit to them. The key to being persuasive is to identify why the person would want to do what you're asking them do. How does it benefit them? Does asking a child to eat their greens help them do the things they want to do? Does asking an employee to work overtime get them one step closer to the promotion they want? Does asking your partner to make you a cup of tea get them a foot rub later that evening? These are trivial examples – but leverage also works on a deeper level. For example, do you have a relationship, say with a friend or a partner, where the leverage is tipped in the other person's favour? If you want to keep that relationship alive, what do you need to do to tip the leverage back in your favour? Can you help them see the value of your relationship by stopping doing some of the things they've become accustomed to? Things like letting them go out every weekend. Having their dinner ready every day. Never voicing your opinion, for the sake of an 'easy' life. If you can't appease them, and if what they want and expect is excessive, unrealistic, makes you unhappy, or shifts the leverage too far in their favour, it's time to walk.

As I mentioned, leverage isn't about bending over backwards to please someone you may never please. The power of leverage should be used when it suits you – to help you balance out relationships and create better circumstances for you.

Don't forget the power of leverage.

The power of influence starts by understanding what the other person wants. Remember: they don't care! You'll struggle to influence anybody if it's all about you. Remember to think 'you', not 'I', and you'll get the outcome you want in any situation. Make sure it's a situation that suits you as much as them, otherwise, the leverage you gain is for nothing.

Influence tool #2:
Be present

Is there anything worse than speaking to somebody who is constantly distracted? They don't make eye contact. They look around. You try to engage them in conversation, only for them to pick up their phone to check their texts midway through your sentence. *Argh!*

You wouldn't take a call in a job interview, because you wouldn't be invited back: 'I'll come back to you on that question about my leadership skills just after I've spoken to my mum. Be back in ten.'

Bad communication is evident in scenarios like job interviews, but lots of us demonstrate bad communication traits all the time.

Persuasion is about *connection* as much as anything else. Someone has to know that they can trust you. You won't persuade someone to do something if they don't trust you. Think of the people you know or you've met who you don't trust. If one of these people asked you to do them a favour, you'd be wary, right? And if they stepped forward to do a favour for you, your first inclination might be to think,

'What's in it for them?' Trust is key, and trust is earned through good communication.

If you're speaking to someone and you're staring straight through them – as if they're invisible – you won't form any type of meaningful connection. The very best communicators and influencers are always present in a conversation, no matter how busy or important they might be. They give their audience their full attention. No matter how much they have on their mind or how they're feeling, they make an effort to show the other person that they're listening and interested. They make eye contact, nod frequently, and make sounds to show interaction and attention. This shows the other person that they're being listened to intently, and that what they're saying is being heard.

Have you noticed the difference between hearing someone and *listening* to what someone is saying? Those two statements sound the same, but they're not. Anyone can hear, but not everyone listens to what is being said. Anyone can be a father, but not everyone is a good dad.

Forming a strong connection and building trust with the people who matter to you is about *listening to what they say*. That means sometimes reading between the lines. When you get better at listening rather than just hearing, you'll build an unbreakable bond. That is the type of bond that takes relationships to new levels. If you can listen to what you partner is saying, your marriage will be solid. If you can listen to what your client is saying, they'll be a client for life.

Everyone's favourite subject is themselves. Sometimes, just listening to someone speak and giving them a little of your attention can make all the difference. Don't underestimate how many bad communicators there are out there, or how quickly you can advance just by listening more. Try it. When you get home from work, put your bag away, hang up your coat, sit down next to your partner and tell them they have your undivided attention. Look at the reaction you get. If anything, maybe the shocked look on their face will amuse you.

If you're not engaged, or are bored by a conversation, do the other person a favour and politely end it. Pretending to be interested is no good for either of you. Your body language and facial expressions will give it away. Have you ever spoken to somebody who came across as fake and inauthentic? It's not a nice trait. You don't want to be put in that category. It's more polite to walk away.

If you're seeing signs that the person you're talking to isn't present, you have a choice: (1) End the conversation and walk away, or (2) Up your game by changing the way you communicate. If it's somebody you want to influence and build a rapport with, try to find some more common ground, and ask more questions. Remember: everyone's favourite subject is themselves. Speaking about themselves will open up most people.

Just remember to strike the balance between caring too much and adopting your 'can't care' mentality. If you find yourself trying to communicate with a bunch of zombies who aren't worth your time, it's time to find another pack. But stay patient – this is ultimately what will make you a master influencer and will tip the balance of leverage in your favour.

Influence tool #3:
Your body

I know I said I'd give you tools that you might not have thought about before – so why am I covering body language when it's obvious? It's because body language is too important to ignore. The smallest, slightest changes in our body language can vastly improve our social confidence and influencing skills.

Your body is speaking for you at all times, even when your mouth isn't moving.

Professor Albert Mehrabian carried out extensive studies on body language in the 1950s, and came up with what is known as the 7% rule. This rule says that only 7% of how we communicate is down to what we say (the words we use); 38% equates to how we say something (including the tone we use); and a whopping 55% represents our non-verbal communication (body language). So, if I told you that you look fantastic while shouting as loudly and aggressively as I could, the compliment is likely to get lost. Ignore body language at your peril!

Unless you're planning to become a body language expert (or an expert at knowing when your partner is lying to you), it's easy to go over the top with studying it. I don't know about you, but I'd much rather enjoy having a conversation with somebody than feel the need to analyse every movement we make. You'd have to become pretty skilled at body language if you're going to be present in a conversation while at the same time analysing what you're both doing.

If you were at a job interview, for example, you could mess it up by concentrating too hard on what you're doing with your hands, eyes and legs than on answering the questions you've been asked. What would the interviewer say? 'It's OK that she didn't answer my questions or listen to me; her hand gestures were fantastic!' I'm pretty sure that wouldn't land you the job.

Instead, let's focus on a few of the most crucial aspects of body language, and aim to get them right. By focusing on these few things, you'll have enough headspace to influence in other areas, like thinking 'you', not 'I', listening well, and being present.

I find that a body map helps keep me focused on the key areas of my body. Let's start from the top and work our way down.

Head and face

Your body language influences your mental state. When you feel down, you portray that in your body language, so you look down. By doing so, you're reinforcing the feeling of being depressed. When you change your body language, you can change how you feel. You send a different message to your brain, which tricks your brain into thinking you're in a better mood. The more you practise changing your body to influence your mood, the better you'll get at it.

What do you do when you feel socially awkward? Apart from hide? You may avoid people and stay in a defensive-type closed position with everything crossed. That will reinforce your feeling of being socially anxious. When you lift your head, uncross your arms, raise your shoulders and puff out your chest, that will change how you feel. It will also change how others perceive you.

Think about your body on a very basic level when it comes to dealing with social anxiety and worrying about what people are thinking about you. How different would you feel if you sat in the same spot allowing all those negative worrying thoughts to hit you, compared to getting up and doing something active, like going to the gym? These are two very different physical states that produce two very different moods. And they are both an option for you.

Here's a great technique to help you remember to keep your head up. (Literally.) Every time you walk through a doorway, put your chin up. Try to associate doorways with lifting your chin. It takes a bit of practice, but the more you make the connection between doorways and keeping your head up, and practise it, the more a doorway will remind you to put your chin up. The more you put your chin up, the more you'll do it without needing a doorway to remind you. You'll also find the rest of your body will follow. For example, when you lift your chin, your shoulders will also naturally lift.

Point your body where you want your mind to go.

You don't have to look like a meerkat on constant alert, but putting your chin up will send your brain a message that you feel confident (even if the reality is different). It will certainly *look* like you're confident.

Also use your head (literally) to influence.

- Use triple nods (nodding quickly three times in a row) when talking and tilt your head slightly when you're listening.
- Lean forward when you're listening.
- Stand up straight when you're speaking.

These are all subtle types of basic body language that help you influence and build an instant rapport.

Eyes

Eyes are the window to the soul. Or, to be more accurate, eyes are the window to your social awkwardness. It's easy to look down and away from people when you feel shy and anxious, which is why eyes are key when it comes to handling social anxiety and awkwardness.

I look into people's eyes to find out what they're thinking, especially when I feel they're not telling me the full story. When I play poker, my opponent's eyes allow me to gauge where I'm at in the hand. (That's why so many poker players wear sunglasses.) We all use eyes to gauge where we stand with somebody. *Are they going to kiss me or slap me?* The eyes never lie. Think about how hard it would be to tell if someone was lying to you if they had their eyes closed. That's how much we depend on eyes when communicating.

Lack of eye contact tends to go hand in hand with social anxiety. It doesn't necessarily signify a lack of respect, but a lack of confidence. Although maintaining eye contact is challenging at times, it's worth making an effort to do it more often to get you a deeper connection. Rather than avoid your boss's stare as he appraises you, look back at him confidently – not in an intense, fixed glare-type stare, though. Give the amount of eye contact that makes everybody feel comfortable. Not enough, and you might come across as unconfident or as if you're not listening. Too much, and you might look like a pyscho! Get the balance right. Think something like 80/20. 80% eye contact, 20% scanning, thinking, and taking in your environment.

'The Power Gaze' is a good technique for eye contact. When you're speaking to someone and you want to appear dominant, or you're in a situation where somebody won't stop talking, rather than make eye contact, imagine a triangle drawn on the person's forehead from the eyes to the top of the forehead. This is the sweet spot. Look there while you're talking and it will make the other person feel under pressure. (Don't use this technique if you're looking for romance or friendship! This is best used in situations where you want to tip the balance of leverage, like when negotiating with a car salesman.)

Ears

You've heard the saying, 'God gave you two ears and one mouth for a reason', right? When I was a kid and not paying attention, I'd hear this a lot. The meaning, of course, is that you should listen more than you talk. And in most circumstances, this is true.

Who do you know who talks a lot? (We all know at least one.) These people are some of the worst communicators you will encounter. Why? Because it's not communication at all! The definition of communication is 'the imparting or exchanging of information by speaking, writing, or using some other medium'. Good communication is about *sharing* information and *listening* to the information being shared. It's two-sided. When you're constantly being talked at, rather than having a conversation, it's annoying. The most patient people will eventually get fed up. Although it's relatively harmless, talking too much is a toxic trait. Go back to some of the solutions and questions in the 'A turd in the punchbowl' chapter if you're facing this dilemma.

Talking is a form of release, which is why most of us like doing it. When we share what's on our mind, it makes us feel better. When we internalise a problem, it makes us feel worse. (A problem shared is a problem halved, after all.) The trouble is, some people have no filter. They forget that other people have problems. These people have few friends, because like I said, eventually, people will move on and make friends with people who want to listen to them, not just talk at them.

I'll repeat a point I made earlier: Everybody's favourite subject is themselves. Whenever you want to start flexing your influencing muscles, just get people taking about themselves. They love it. Ask them what they like and why they like it. Treat them as if they're the most fascinating person you've ever met. They'll love you. This is one of the most effective rapport-building and ice-breaking techniques you can use. Dale Carnegie, the author of *How to Win Friends and Influence People*, said you can make more friends in two months by becoming truly interested in other people than you can in two years by trying to get other people interested in you.

You're on to a winner when the person reciprocates by asking about you. You've then got a free-flowing two-way conversation between two skilled communicators who not only know how to talk, but also know how to use their ears and listen. Perfect!

Mouth and smile

Socially anxious people don't smile. Socially confident people smile – a lot. Not necessarily because they're always happy, but because they know the power behind a smile. Smiling shows the world you're ready for it. It shows others that you're approachable, and that you're happy to see them (even if that's not always the case!).

When you smile at somebody, they usually smile back. That creates a nice cycle of positivity. Be careful not to offer a half-arsed fake smile – one where your mouth goes up at the corners but your eyes stay in the same position. If you're going to smile, do it properly. Show some teeth! Smiling is another instant rapport-builder.

Hands

Let's start with a handshake, because first impressions count! Have you heard of the phrase 'he's got a wet fish handshake'? Apart from garlic breath, a wet fish handshake is one of the worst things you can be presented with when you meet someone. The hand is extended in a limp fashion and the receiver holds on to it, like holding onto a wet fish. It's double trouble when the hand is sweaty!

Just as bad as the wet fish is the hand-crusher. If you crush a person's hand with Hulk-like force, it's not good. Has someone shaken your hand like that? The next five minutes of your conversation are dominated by you thinking how much a dick he is, and wondering if he has broken any bones. Aim to match the other person's grip for the best rapport. (Don't end up in A&E with broken bones if you're both hand-crushers.)

If you feel your hand getting a little sweaty, maybe when you're nervous before a job interview, make sure your hands aren't wet by giving them a wipe and keeping them open to allow the air to get to them. Give them a discreet blow to keep them dry while you wait. Nobody likes a sweaty handshake...

Arms and legs
Most people know we use crossed arms as a defence mechanism. It's a popular stance when we feel socially anxious. Our arms act as a 'barrier' in a social situation. Whether or not we want to show it, crossing our arms is defensive. If you're having a conversation with somebody, you're basically telling them you don't want to talk to them,

or you're bored with what they're saying. If you're in a group of people, when you cross your arms you're signifying you don't want to be there. That might not be true, but your body is doing all the talking for you. That is how people will see it. It's one of the quickest ways to break down rapport.

Crossing your legs is commonly used for comfort (especially for women). It doesn't signify negativity as much as crossing arms.

To build and keep a rapport and show social confidence, wherever possible, keep your body nice and open. Show others how approachable and friendly you are by opening your arms and hands (I was reluctant to write 'legs' here) and inviting them into your space. People will instantly warm to you, and they'll be ready to spark up a conversation with you.

Influence tool #4:
Get involved

I used to hate social events, and I'd avoid them like the plague. Parties, weddings: you name it, I'd avoid it. On the rare occasion I'd put my social anxiety aside and I ended up going out, my insecurity at the event manifested itself as silence. I was as quiet as a mouse. You wouldn't know I was there. I'd be the one sitting far outside the social circle so I didn't have to make conversation, avoiding all eye and physical contact. Looking back, this was sad. I not only missed out on a lot of joy, but I also completely misrepresented who I was (my true self).

Although I wasn't aware of it at the time, people paid attention to my silence. After the event, my partner would get comments like 'Your partner is quiet, isn't he?' and 'He looked like he didn't want to be there'. They thought I was arrogant and rude, but the truth was, I was shy and not very confident. Maybe you do this yourself? Maybe you've seen other people doing it? When you start paying attention, you'll notice that most social gatherings follow the same theme. You get the 'shouters'. There is usually at least one at a party. Then you get the 'minglers'. These people are happy chatting away and socialising all night. Then you get the 'outsiders'. These people are always on the fringe of the social circle, avoiding human contact where possible. It's the outsiders who are most misunderstood.

The outsiders look like they're doing it because they don't care. If they have the outward appearance of someone who should be confident, they might also be viewed as being arrogant and rude. But you'll find that most of these people are unconfident and shy. They actually care the most. When you get talking to them – because it is someone else who has to spark the conversation – you'll find they're not the arrogant, ignorant person you thought they were. They just needed a little nudge to get them going in the right direction.

If you are this person, your silence and lack of interaction are being noted. Whether or not you want to interact, or feel it's unfair to be judged if you don't, you're still being judged. You're also potentially misrepresenting yourself as someone who is arrogant and rude. You can't care about that. What I'm bothered about here is *you* feeling better in a social environment. However you look at it, sitting uncomfortably outside the social circle because of shyness isn't a pleasant experience. You deserve more, and you should be able to get involved without being crippled by nerves. There are two things you can do to resolve this.

1. Decide that social events just aren't worth the hassle and don't go to any more, no matter the pressure

friends and family put on you to go. Close yourself off to society and become a recluse.
2. Get involved.

I don't take point one lightly, and I don't want to come across as flippant. I know first-hand what it's like to have social anxiety so bad that just the thought of a wedding sends shivers down my spine. I became socially isolated and housebound, so I know exactly how it feels. I included option one because it is a choice. There's little point putting yourself through a social situation if you're not willing to put some effort into changing your behaviour. If you enter a social environment with the intention of staying quiet and sitting outside the social circle, why are you bothering? The only reason you're going is to please other people. You've just read a book on why this is a bad idea!

I hope you're much more likely to pick option two, and get involved. Ultimately, that's what will help you improve your social and influencing skills. It's all about practice, and you can't practise getting it right unless you're willing to give it a go and get involved. If you keep going to social events and sitting outside the social circle, all you're doing is practising how to look and feel uncomfortable – and you'll continue to get good at it! So the first part of fixing this is to change your mindset about what a social environment is. It's nothing more than a meeting of minds – between people with different views, looks, attitudes and opinions. That's it.

Please remember: When it comes to social anxiety, the worst part of any social event is your worry before the actual event! It's the 'what ifs': 'What if I make a fool of myself?' 'What if I'm not interesting enough?' 'What if they hate me?' We catastrophise and make up endless stories in our head about falling onto the cake and tripping up on the dance floor. By the time you've spent three months worrying about it, no wonder you don't want to go! It's your survival instinct working against you again. Your brain creates the worst-case scenario because it thinks it's protecting you. But all it's doing is stopping you from living. Ignore your brain. Think about all the worrying thoughts you have in one day. Go one step further and actually write them down. When you look at them, you'll see that the worst-case scenario is rarely ever close to being reality.

Once you're at the event, focus on talking and getting involved. When you break through the fear, you'll realise all these 'what ifs...' were just negative self-talk designed to keep you isolated and trapped. You'll soon appreciate that other people are just as nervous and as unconfident as you are; they just mask it better by getting involved. You might even enjoy yourself!

Social isolation is not healthy for anyone. Option one is for quitters. You're not a quitter. You've demonstrated that by getting this far in the book. Avoid avoidance, and start saying yes. Go and get involved. You won't regret it.

Change is good

Your 'can't care' mentality is taking shape. Your authentic social confidence is growing, and you're feeling better about being true to yourself and being who you really are. All of this has been made possible because you are open to change. That makes me happy. Why? Because the thought of change can induce feelings of fear – fear that prevents us from taking action and making change.

If this fear is still hounding you, and you're scared you're not going to have your breakthrough because of it, I have some comfort for you. There is only one other thing as certain as death and taxes, and that thing is *change*. Change is so inevitable that they should change that popular saying to include it. I'd like you to start embracing the fact that change is inevitable and constant, and not be scared of it. *Change is good.*

Even if it feels like your life has become monotonous, nothing ever stays the same. Everything is always changing – including you. When you feel stuck and like your social anxiety isn't changing, remember that all it takes is a few steps in a different direction to get that change going.

We're creatures of habit. That makes significant change easier said than done. Brands know this. How difficult do you find it to buy a different brand of a product you use, even if you don't think it's as good as it used to be? We do the same thing with habits and beliefs. We hold on tight to them, even if they're no good for us. Habits like using pretence and fakery to get people to like us. Although these things just lead to social anxiety, insecurity, worry and doubt, we've programmed ourselves to think that's the norm. We feel comfortable with the familiarity of doing it, even if that familiarity leads to a crappy existence. We don't realise that the comfort created by familiarity is what's keeping us trapped. We've got to start getting more aware of these habits and behaviours so we can do something about them, rather than let them dominate who we are.

I work on the principle: *If you knew me yesterday, you don't know me today.* If you have to change something, don't mess around – change it. If you put up with something you weren't happy with yesterday, don't do it again today. If you do, you'll get the same result you got yesterday. Nothing will change. Your life will stay the same. You will be the same. You'll *feel* the same.

If you want something different, like more respect, you have to do something different to get it.

Life is way too short to mess around. That famous Spanish response used by builders halfway through their job sums it up: *mañana*. (For the non-Spanish speakers, it means 'tomorrow'.) Tomorrow comes and the shower and toilet still aren't plumbed in. You still have to go to your friend's house to use their facilities. The trouble is, if you let him, the builder will keep getting away with his shoddy timekeeping. Your friend will get fed up with you using their house as a hotel. You'll get used to putting up with it all – all because you didn't have the balls to act.

'I haven't got time now. I'll change it tomorrow.'

'I'll do the overtime this week, but it will be the last time. I'll tell my boss I'm not doing overtime next time.'

'I'll leave him the next time he abuses me. He'd better not do it a fifteenth time.'

'I'll end the relationship when the timing is right. He needs me. I'll break his heart if I leave him now.'

I hate to break it to you, but the timing will never be right. Tomorrow never comes. **The moment is now**.

Don't be afraid to seize the moment. Don't be afraid of change. *Change is good*. Life is about growth. You can't grow without change. If you're not growing, you're dying. If you don't grow, you'll put off every task you promise yourself you'll get round to doing. You will continue to be the one your boss targets to do overtime. Your partner will continue to abuse you. You will stay in a dead-end relationship because of guilt. You will be shackled by your constant need for everyone's approval.

Act today. Act now. **And don't stop taking action.**

People (especially the people closest to you) will be shocked by your change in attitude. They'll raise their eyebrows when you step forward and take the lead. They'll get confused by the fact that they can't say and do the same things that they did to you yesterday. Good. That is excellent feedback for you. That means that you are growing. It means that you are no longer prepared to settle for anything less than your new standards. It means you are no longer willing to take BS. It means that you are prepared to do what is necessary to grow. If they don't like the new you, that's not your concern. You can't care about that. If anything, it raises a question mark over whether or not they were good for your life anyway. If someone can't handle your ability to change, and makes no effort to change or improve themselves, that is not your problem.

Ask for help

On your journey, don't be afraid to ask for help. You can't be expected to do everything yourself. Sometimes you need a helping hand, and that's OK. When your car breaks down, assuming you're not a mechanic, you'll need help to identify and fix the problem. The mechanic will find the cause of the problem so you can fix it quickly. Think the same way about other, less obvious, problems in your life, like a lack of confidence. There are people out there who can help, including coaches like me.

Although seeking help from others might sound counterproductive to self-confidence and independence, it's not. Authentically confident people consistently ask for help. There is no weakness or shame in putting your hand up when you need to. It's sometimes the fastest route to getting to where you want to be. Insecure people try to hide their inability to do something, and they will continue to struggle. Think about why you picked up this book. It was a way for you to ask for help. Don't be afraid of that. You can't care about people who find helping themselves – in the form of self-help and coaching – a joke. Keep reading and educating yourself. It's your route to higher levels of self-awareness, with each step providing a new experience.

If you're naturally independent, like me, you might struggle with the concept of asking for help. But you have to develop this habit if you want to progress quicker. You could spend a lot of time trying to solve a problem when one call to a friend or professional might be all it takes. That's why the most successful people on the planet have an extensive network of contacts. When they need help, they usually have an expert they can call for advice.

The moral of the story here is to stop doing everything yourself. It's impossible – and, ultimately, it's only holding you back. Sometimes you have to swallow your pride and say, 'I need help'. The more you do it, the more comfortable you'll feel asking for help in the future, and the more your pride will get buried – which is only a good thing. It's the bad side of your pride that brings out all your social anxieties and insecurities so, ideally, we want it residing next to the *Titanic*.

However, asking for help doesn't mean not taking responsibility. It's not about delegating all your problems and expecting them to go away. You have to be able to help yourself first before expecting anyone else to help you.

That means taking responsibility for your problems, and taking action on them – today.

It's up to you to change something if you want it changed. Nobody else is going to do it for you. If someone has spoken to you like you're a piece of crap for a decade, they're not going to stop unless *you* change the situation. You can ask them to stop, but you can't expect to control them. **Only you can change the situation.** Only you can say 'I've had enough' and decide what you want to do. You're in control. Don't ever forget that. No matter how rude someone is to you, and how small they make you feel, **you always have a choice.**

Authentic confidence is a lot like money. If you wait for it to come to you, you'll be waiting for a long time. The more you wait for it, the more of it you will spend, and the less of it you'll get. (Reread that bit.) Why should your new 'can't care' mentality take weeks, months, years or even decades to start, when you can start implementing changes instantly? Start today!

You've just had a book-full of new knowledge. But knowledge is only *potential* power. **Knowledge becomes powerful when you're taking daily *action*.**

I want your newfound authentic confidence to continue to grow and last a lifetime. I don't want the knowledge in this book to be a quick fix for the next important decision you have to make. I want all your future decisions to come from an authentic place of confidence. Feel free to read a hundred more books, but if you don't decide to take action, your reading has been for nothing. True power comes from taking consistent, daily action. Inaction is the cause of all your issues. Action is the cure-all – social anxiety included.

How do I take action?

Start by deciding what you're not happy about. These things cause you negative feelings, and lead to social anxiety, resentment and anger. These are things that keep you trapped and awake at night. They play on your subconscious because you know something isn't quite right. These are the things in your life that need fixing. They are your starting point for action and change.

Grab a pen and a piece of paper and write them down. There is something powerful about getting your thoughts out of your head and on paper. If you need a little inspiration, here are some suggestions.

- A friend or family member who treats you like a doormat.
- A partner who abuses you.
- A boss who doesn't respect you.
- A people-pleasing habit or behaviour.
- An old belief that is keeping you trapped and in fear.

Next, decide what you need to do to change the situation. To help, ask yourself the questions we asked previously:

- Can you forgive them for what they've done?
- Are you sad when you're not with them?
- Does it hurt your pride to think you have to make the first move?
- Do they make you feel guilty?
- Are you less or more effective without them?

You might not be able to change some of these things overnight, but you can decide that they *will* change – and you can do that instantly. The decision to act, combined with the first small step (action), is all it takes. The step can be as small as you like, because you can guarantee this: When you've completed that step, you will take another step, and another. Momentum will build and lead to further action. Taking action will be your new behaviour and habit. And that ain't a bad habit to have.

When it comes to making changes, the fear of change makes us focus on all the negatives. That includes all the things we think we haven't done or achieved. Think about all the things you've done and achieved in your life. When you think about it, there's a lot. Don't be modest – give yourself credit. You've already got through the problems you've faced. How did you do this? *By starting!* The worst part of going to the gym is getting there. The hardest part of a DIY project is starting it. The most difficult stage of overcoming social anxiety, worry, insecurity and self-doubt is choosing to change it all by switching your mentality.

Your brain is marvellous. (I've just given you a backhanded compliment, because I'm basically saying that *you* are marvellous.) When you choose to switch to your new 'can't care' mentality, your brain will give you solutions. First, you've got to be OK with presenting your brain with these challenges. Don't hide away from them. Put some trust in yourself. You'll come up with the answers. When you feel stuck, look for answers and knowledge. They'll come to you. When they do, take action. Don't let the opportunity pass you by. Don't say 'I'll do it tomorrow'. Take responsibility, and take action – *today.*

While you're taking action, don't forget what a 'can't care' mentality means:

- You're not led by fear or ego.
- You're self-aware.
- You use emotion *and* logic.
- You give yourself time to reflect.
- You choose comfort over conformity.
- You don't compare yourself with other people.
- You're comfortable with being judged.
- You deal with your inner voice when it lies.
- You know nobody cares – and that's good!
- You view everyone as human.
- You're happy to step outside your comfort zone and grow.

There will be people who will try to clip your wings. Keep taking action, and eventually you'll soar so high that they can't reach you. You have chosen to get educated. You have made the choice to become more self-aware. You have decided to deal with social anxiety, including your worry about what people think of you, in a different way. Good for you, my friend. Please, go and use your newfound freedom. Embrace it.

Keep your beautiful mind free, and don't be a prisoner ever again.

1-2-1 Coaching

As a personal coach, I've worked with thousands of individuals, all with unique goals and ambitions.

I empower my clients to overcome anxiety and stress-related conditions, freeing them from their crippling, debilitating effects.

If you are dealing with anxiety or stress and you think coaching will help, get in touch.

You can find my contact details on my website.

www.carlvernon.com

Stay in touch

You can stay in touch with me on my website:

www.carlvernon.com

There you'll find more information on what I offer, including workshops, coaching, my podcast and blog – all to help you can't care.

Take care and best wishes,

Carl Vernon

Printed in Great
Britain
by Amazon